500 SONGWRITING IDEAS

(For Brave and Passionate People)

by Lisa Aschmann

6400 Hollis Street
Emeryville, CA 94608

Library of Congress Catalog Card Number: 97-71391

Book design and layout: Linda Gough
Front cover art: Amelia Louise Hogan
Front cover design: Linda Gough

Production staff: Mike Lawson: publisher; Lisa Duran: editor;
Randy Antin: editorial assistant; Sally Engelfried: editorial assistance;
Teresa Poss: administrative assistant; Ellen Richman: production director;
Tom Marzella: production assistant

6400 Hollis Street
Emeryville, CA 94608
(510) 653-3307

Also from MixBooks:
Music Publishing: The Real Road to Music Business Success, Rev. and Exp. 4th Ed.
How to Run a Recording Session
The Songwriters Guide to Collaboration, Rev. and Exp. 2nd Ed.
Critical Listening and Auditory Perception
Keyfax Omnibus Edition
The AudioPro Home Recording Course
Modular Digital Multitracks: The Power User's Guide
Concert Sound
Sound for Picture
Music Producers
Live Sound Reinforcement

Also from EMBooks:
Making the Ultimate Demo
Tech Terms: A Practical Dictionary for Audio and Music Production
Making Music With Your Computer

Also from CBM Music and Entertainment Group:
Recording Industry Sourcebook
Mix Reference Disc
Mix Master Directory
Digital Piano Buyer's Guide

MixBooks is a division of Cardinal Business Media Inc.

Printed in Auburn Hills, Michigan

ISBN 0-918371-15-5

Contents

Preface

One of the most pernicious words in the English language, in my view, is "genius." Another one is "talent." These words divide people and keep them from accessing what is native to them: their own creativity. Genius mystifies what is readily available. Creativity is an immediately accessible, widely distributed birthright. People are smart, but they're afraid to look dumb. And they think that others, unlike themselves, have something special. They think that they require something special, some prerequisite skill/talent/genius before they can give themselves permission to let go and let their ideas flow freely. They let their editor/critic/censor kick in before they just *do* it: problem solve and generate new songs. It doesn't work like that. Be fearless. Be thought inept, crazy, foolish, and a terrible writer or musician. Let them laugh but write anyway. My motto is: Dare to be stupid.

It's not that I believe in or endorse stupidity. It's the *daring* that counts. Fear is the gatekeeper to the floodgates of inspiration. Also, "beginner mind," an attitude of ignorance, is useful. The best inoculation from learning something is knowing it already. So, dare to begin and begin again. There are two main impediments to being creative. One is being overly critical. The other is being overly awed. (Being overly odd may help.) But if we're all down here making monkeys of ourselves and ordinary mortals write songs, then you, too, can dare to be stupid.

Anybody can write songs. Especially, brave and passionate people can write songs. People like us risk looking stupid in order to create something new. Our love of music is stronger than our fear of rejection.

These are creativity exercises. Some suggestions have to do with music, others have to do with language, still others have to do with loosening up, and some have to do with finding inspiration in what others have done before you. Keeping an open mind is good for songwriting, even if that means sometimes restricting yourself to some tried and true forms. As Maya Angelou says, "I know why the caged bird sings." So do I; it's *because* of the cage, not in spite of it. Creativity is set free within the confines of form and game playing. Lighten up. These are arbitrary, silly exercises.

Face it, you're going to have to write some duds to get to the gems. I figure I'm well into the first phase of this, so any day now I might write a keeper. Go, thou, and do likewise.

Acknowledgments

I'd like to thank (so I'm going to) the staff and students of the Puget Sound Guitar Workshop (PSGW), especially John Miller, Becky and John Knowles, Ray Bierl, Bob Brozman, Joe Vinikow, Chris Grampp, Peter Langston, Kim Scanlon, Tom Rawson, Marcia Taylor, Daniel Steinberg, and Janet Peterson, for putting bees in my bonnet and helping me get started; Larry Joba for typing this; and other friends and writers for their creativity, such as Elaine Farris Hughes, Buddy Kaye, Dick Goodwin, Rick Beresford, K.A. Parker, Cat Cohen, Janis Stevenson, Doug Hall, and Steve Gillette. This started out as class material for the Puget Sound Guitar Workshop and sort of mushroomed. It's a good climate for mushrooms up there on the Olympic Peninsula . . .

I don't even play an instrument, and I've written 2,000 songs. My friends are the reasons why. Bill Piburn, Jamey Whiting, Jim Lewin, John Haley-Walker, Catesby Jones, Joel Evans, David Toby, Michael Johnson, Pat Bergeson, Rick Dougherty, Don Carlisle, Scott Musick, Ron Troutman, John Smith, Kerry Marx, Fred Koller, Frank Baldwin, David West, Joel Plimmer, Jerry Styner, John Tirro, Richard Follett, Michael Lounibos, Jack Fischer, Rolf Wyer, Jeff Lewis, David Vasquez, Gary Pickus, Larry Batiste, Jack Pearson, Lindy Hearne, Ron Kristy, Bob Patin, Bobby Pinson, Dorian Michaels, David Alexander, Michael Behymer, Tom Kimmel, Michael Lille, Mike Williams, Paul Alan Smith, Mark Burchfield, Jim Burrill, Henry Hipkens, Kent Blazy, Woody Mann, John Mock, Roger Day, David Bartky, Steve Parrish, Tim Johnson, Tim Mathews, Dan Marcus, Jimmy Jackson, Rick Ryan, Barry Fasman, Wayne Carson, Mark Simos, Robert Berry, Tom Doty, Dan E. Strymer, Howard Schwartz, Tom Fox, Michael Harmon, Kevin Carr, Tom Paxton, Roger Linn, Bob Reid, Ray Frank, Danny Timms—and *so* on, the list goes on and on—Joni Bishop, Nancy Conescu, Joyce Woodson, Betsy Jackson, Marilyn Hencken, Sandy Sherman, Lena Lucas, Jane Murray, Kate Wallace, Francis Glascoe, Helen White, Karen Taylor Good, Sally Barris, Carol Hashe, Ellen Daros, jael, Ellen Britton, Lynn Langham, Lynne Robin Green, Barbara Mendelsohn, Karee Wardrop, Cee Jay McDuffy, Piper Heisig, Noel Cash, Joyce Rouse, Sonny Ochs, Patti and Michael Silversher—oh, it could go on a long time, this list! These people have co-written and arranged and backed me up and encouraged me like nobody's business and respected me and my musical ideas, too. It takes a genuinely great spirit to let somebody learn on your time. Thanks, you guys!

Larry Joba, my hero, worked like a navvy on this, typing, getting permission to use quotes, and checking references. Thank you, Larry! Special thanks are due my daughter Amelia for the cover art and to all my children for staying off the computer while all this was going on. And thanks to Lisa Duran and the staff of MixBooks for staying on through the same.

As this is a book on songwriting, I've tried to give credit to the writers of the songs I mention. I thank—we all thank—them for their wonderful songs. On the other hand, I apologize if I have omitted or made mistakes in attribution. This is just part of my mental library, and some of the shelves are pretty empty. Sorry! It's a tribute to these songs that the very mention of a title or a line from them is recognizable, and as such, there really is no losing sight of their origins. That certainly wasn't intended.

My thank-yous wouldn't be complete without mentioning two of my co-writers in memoriam, Georgia Yates and Molly Finkle, two fine lyricists in the Bay Area. As Georgia used to ask when I walked into the room, "What's *on?* Your *mind?*

500
Songwriting
Ideas

*Dare to be stupid. A thing worth
doing is worth doing anyway.*

1

Turn off the sound on the TV and write
conversations for the soap operas.

2

Eavesdrop at a cafe.

3

Study advertisements. How is something bigger, newer,
more compact, faster? How is pleasure promised?
How is "better" shown?

4

Make up life stories of people in stores,
airports, or bus terminals.

5

Plan a series of sermons or lessons about life.
Finish these phrases:
_____ when all else fails.
The first/last thing my mom/dad told me was_____.
I was born to _____.
You can always count on _____ to _____.
I wouldn't trade a million bucks for _____.

6

Imagine that body parts or household objects have feelings. What would this
door, mirror, table, picture, heart, wall say if it could talk?

7

Imitate the rhythms of nursery rhymes, e.g.,
"Jack Sprat could eat no fat . . ." "Ride a cock horse to Banbury Cross . . ."
"Little Miss Muffet sat on a tuffet . . . "

8

Translate poetry from a language you don't know.

9

Fracture some fairy tales. Retell a movie plot.

10

Explain earthlings to aliens; what are our customs for?

11

What would you like to tell your hero/favorite teacher/child? Write an
important letter to someone you know.

12

Define these terms: home, a life worth living, the perfect day, what I want most, the greatest gift, my dream lover.

13

Use counterfactuals. If _____ weren't true, then I'd be a monkey's uncle, e.g., "Till the Rivers All Run Dry" (Don Williams and Wayland Holyfield), "If Ever I Would Leave You" (Alan Jay Lerner and Frederick Loewe), ("I've got some") "Ocean Front Property" ("in Arizona . . . ") (Garland Cochran, Royce Porter, and Dean Dillon).

14

Create switcheroos, e.g., "Not only are things seldom what they seem, but they never were" (Marshall Barer). Look for true paradoxes, opposites, contrasts, e.g., "Up is Down" (Marshall Barer), "Full Moon and Empty Arms" (Buddy Kaye and Ted Mossman), "Come Rain or Come Shine" (Johnny Mercer and Harold Arlen), "The Night We Called It a Day" (Thomas Adair and Matt Dennis), "The Last Thing I Needed the First Thing This Morning . . . " (Gary P. Nunn and Sam Farar).

15

Make lists of synonyms, metaphors, and similes and use them to create titles or first lines. A good exercise to do along these lines is to finish the phrase "as quiet as a _____," and don't say "mouse"; "as hard as a _____," and don't say "rock"; as light as a _____," and don't say "feather," etc.

16

List things that go together, e.g., socks and shoes, salt and pepper, "Leather and Lace" (Graeme Pleeth), "We Were Meant to Be Together" (Jeffrey Taylor), "Scotch and Soda" (Dave Guard).

17

Count things, e.g., "Eighteen Wheels and a Dozen Roses" (Paul Nelson and Gene Nelson), "The 12 Days of Christmas," "If the Devil Danced" ("in empty pockets, he'd have a ball in mine, with a 9-foot grand, a 10-piece band, and a 12-foot chorus line . . .") (Kim Williams and Ken Spooner). There are 88 keys on a piano, 4 quarts in a gallon, 2-lane highways, a first and last what?

18

List the best of things, e.g., Cole Porter's "You're the Top," "Cadillac Style" (Mark Petersen), "You Take the Cake" (Joseph Garland), Godiva chocolates.

19

Use onomatopoeia, sounds that "say themselves": RRRRRING, BEEEEEP, BLAM! For instance, you could imitate a train whistle as Tom Kimmel does in his song "Blue Train," which he wrote with Jennifer Kimball. Repetition of certain syllables can make flute-like, bell-like, or train-like sounds; e.g., "piccolo meeny" sounds like a piccolo when repeated fast and high. "Chicken fricassee" or "a ticket in a pocket" when repeated can sound like train wheels. Some three-part rounds or spoken pieces are designed with that effect in mind, e.g., "Soup," "One Bottle of Pop," etc.

20

What does nature sound like? For instance, "The wind in the willows, sighing like a solitary soul alone . . . "

21

Write about a favorite city, state, place. Use qualities of the place to describe a person or a feeling, e.g., Hoagy Carmichael and Stuart Gorrell's "Georgia on My Mind."

22

Walk. Walk in different rhythms. Two-step, waltz, tap your feet, slide, run, spin, clap your hands, wave your arms, wag your head. Get funky and see what song suggests itself to you.

23

Write twenty ways to say "I Love You" without using the word "love"
and twenty ways to say "good-bye" without saying "good-bye."

24

Make exceptions without using the word "but."

25

Motivate somebody to rebel against something.

26

What's the hardest thing you ever did? The easiest? What's your proudest
moment? Your saddest moment? Go inward.

27

Pick somebody you admire and write about them.

28

Put music to different art forms. What would a Paul Klee sing like?
A Vermeer? What is Rodin's *The Thinker* pondering?

29

Try intervals you've never tried before, even weird ones, like $1 \to 9$
(e.g. "Walk Against the Wind" [Lisa Aschmann and David Bartky]);
or start with melodic tension that needs to be resolved, like Leonard
Bernstein's "Maria" $1 \to 5^\flat \to 5$.

30

Stick to a genre. Try a traditional twelve-bar blues, dominant sevenths
(four bars each of $1^{7\flat}, 4^{7\flat}, 5^{7\flat}, 1^{7\flat}, 4^{7\flat}, 1^{7\flat}$), a ragtime feel,
a reggae feel, or a bossa nova piece.

31

Write a canon or a round.

32

Illustrate a musical theory idea in a song. Examples: "Circle of Fifths"
(Raun McKinnon) or "One Note Samba" (Antonio Carlos Jobim).

33

Write a song for an occasion. Birthdays and christenings are
good, as are weddings, farewells, and holidays. Or make up
a holiday, call it by your own name, and say what you do to
celebrate it.

34

Imitate a group's style. Write a newly discovered Beatles tune or an Andrews
Sisters or Beach Boys song. Parody not only their lyrical style, but their
harmony styles, e.g., "We Are Not Crosby, Stills, Nash, and Young" by RST.

35

Pick a rhythmic nonsense word or phrase and make it a centerpiece, e.g.,
"Diddy Wah Diddy" (Leon Redbone), "Da Doo Ron Ron" (Jeff Barry, Ellie
Greenwich, and Phil Spector), fol de rol de rincum caddie, etc.

36.

Make a list of your favorite words or the prettiest sounds you know and see if
you can work them into a song somehow. Do that with your favorite chord
progressions, etc.

37

Remember what bugs you about certain people? Tell them off.

38

Have a dialogue with a kid. Sample topics: Why is the sky blue?
Why did he/she/it have to die? What is the color of love?
Where do you go when you're asleep?

39

Tell a tall tale, e.g., "Darby Ram." Make it a whopper but try to make it
plausible. For instance: That winter, we were so hungry we ate our words.
That summer, it was so hot corn popped in the field.

40

You've met a genie. What are your three wishes?

41

You've met the Dalai Lama. What did he say? (I know what *you* say;
you say, "Hello, Dolly!" [Jerry Herman].)

42

You've met your favorite actor or author. What do you do together?

43

Write in one of the modes you don't usually hear—e.g., Aeolian (minor),
Dorian (Celtic)—or use a harmonic minor key (e.g., Aeolian) but sharp
the 7th or make the leading tone an augmented 2nd. In other words,
alter a mode with accidentals to create special scales to give your
music that flamenco or gypsy effect.

44

Adopt the point of view and voice of the opposite sex,
and write from that perspective.

45

Think about why you believe or don't believe in God.
Tell the story of how you came to believe or not believe.

46

Sing a song for your enemy. Who or what do you hate the most?
Write about getting rid of it. Write about your own freedom.

47

Spell out the reasons why you stopped doing something you used to do.

48

Pick a pet or totem animal to honor.

49

Take us on a journey.

50

Write about a season of the year or a certain month.

51

What are your waking rituals and thoughts, your first, your last?
Any prayers? Did you know you could *sing* grace before a meal?

52

Take a mental photograph. Pretend you're a movie camera. Pick a scene that
has a process going on in it already, like a rodeo or a Coca Cola bottling plant
work day, where you could shoot from one angle indefinitely. Then play with
camera conventions—freeze-frame, zoom lens, close-up, fisheye, fast forward,
time lapse, flashback—and edit the scene. What if you could film something
important in your life? What's different about TV versus reality? Headline the
events you see. Parody journalistic style.

53

Write about inner versus outer experiences (i.e., what you say
versus what you don't say in any given social scene), for example,
"The Waltz," a short story by Dorothy Parker.

54

Try writing a story or a musical piece backward.

55

Write a musical palindrome.

56

Write your phone number, the Fibonacci series, Avogadro's number, pi, e,
Planck's constant, license plates, street addresses, letters as numbers (1-26). In
other words, randomize a sequence of notes or chords.

57

Make up a word and write about what it means. Start a gibberish conversation.

58

Mentally visit a carnival, museum, mental hospital, or zoo and tell about the
exhibits, the experience, the crowd. Then, write about the widest, most open
spaces you can think of, like the prairies, Alpha Centauri, etc.

59

Play with irony and sincerity. Write a heartfelt song and a really sarcastic one.

60

Write music over "Heart and Soul" (1 6 4 5 chords). This song by
Hoagy Carmichael and Frank Loesser may be a great one, but it isn't
the only great one, now is it?

61

If you weren't you, who would you be? Write about that person.

62

If there were a moon colony or a Martian colony,
what would its national anthem sound like?

63

Write songs for stereotypical characters, like the hunk, the sex kitten, the old
maid, the hustler, the innocent, the criminal, the cheater, the bartender, the
night clerk, the taxi driver, the big spender (or use several in one song).

64

Imagine being sunlight or water.

65

Whatever happened to your first love? Tell the story or make up a
story about what happened years later.

66

Think about the ground. How does it look in your hand? Underfoot? In an
earthquake? An excavation? A garden? A farm? A rocky mountain top?
Remember the last time you were really in touch with the earth. How did it
feel? How about asphalt? Concrete? Write a song for one of these landscapes:
the Alps, the Grand Canyon, the Everglades.

67

Write a song that you would have to whisper.

68

Write a song with the word "heart," "night," or "if" in the title. These are the
three most often used words in hit song titles.

69

Write a heartfelt, emotional song without using the words
"love," "heart," or "feel."

70

Write a kid's song to teach counting or the alphabet.

71

Write a funny song; see if you can make the listener laugh.

72

Talk about aging from the point of view of regret (lost youth, etc.), rebellion,
pity, or admiration, e.g., "Nick of Time" by Bonnie Raitt.

73

Write a song from a book or movie title.

74

Write a song titled a man or woman's name and really
make them come alive as a character study. For example,
"Bad, Bad Leroy Brown" by Jim Croce.

75

Where would I be without you? Finish:
If it weren't for _____,
I'd be _____.

76

Where are you most at peace?

77

Systematically take all of the intellect out of your song idea. As I heard a producer complain to a singer recently when he wanted him to re-sing a line: "Hey, I hear you *thinking* in there!" What he meant was get out of your head and into your heart. Scan what you're doing for intellectual versus emotional impact. What's left after you *quit* thinking?

78

Pick objects that aggravate you and put them in the center of your song.

79

Try writing five kinds of love songs
with you and your (real or ideal) lover in mind.
(The most common type is #4.)
1. Write about the lover in the first person,
   e.g., "He's So Shy" (Tom Snow and Cynthia Weil).
2. Write about the lover in the second person,
   for example, "Tell Laura I Love Her"
   by Jeff Barry and Ben Raleigh.
3. Write about the lover in the third person,
   for instance, "She's in Love With the Boy"
   (Jon Ims).
4. Write to the lover from the first person,
   e.g., Billy Joel's ("I love you") "Just the Way
   You Are."
5. Write about the relationship in first person plural.
   Examples: "We Belong" (Eric Lowen and
   Dan Navarro) and "Look at Us" (Vince Gill).

80

Here are some adjectives about love:

immature/mature	fiery
celestial	star-crossed
divine	illicit
passionate	devoted
brotherly	suffocating
obsessive	honest
ravenous	embracing
rapturous	delirious
magnificent	powerful
endless	innocent
tender	wild

What others can you think of?

81

Is it stale or is it style? Ask your friends to point out when your music "all sounds the same," then look for fresh material. Or see if you can develop a really exact style for yourself by staying with similar topics, chord progressions, line lengths, grooves, etc.

82

Flip Breskin collects songs she calls "songs of compassion." Yes! Write one of these. What do your feet tell you after you've walked a mile in somebody else's moccasins?

83

Finish these phrases:

The only thing I care about is _____.

All I ever wanted was _____.

_____ is all I need.

_____ is all I've got left.

_____ is what I'm living for.

_____ means everything to me.

I've waited a lifetime for _____.

_____ is the most important thing in the world to me.

I'll be _____ as long as I have _____.

84

The bad news *is* the good news. Find some examples of this, e.g., Uncle Harry died and left you a million bucks.

85

Write a song about a job or an occupation, for example, "Drill Ye Tarriers, Drill."

86

Write about your heritage, your roots, the land(s) of your forefathers and foremothers.

87

Here's a romantic triangle plot: Boy meets girl; girl falls in love with boy's best friend. Write about sexual jealousy, betrayal, friendship, choices.

88

Write a series of negative injunctions:

Don't _____.

I'm not _____.

Note, though, that when you do this, you introduce the idea you're trying to negate. "Don't think of a camel" is a great way to get somebody to visualize a camel. And what about "I'm Not in Love" (David Byrne) or ("I ain't") "Missing You" (John Waite, Mark Leonard, and Charles Sandford)? Who believes them?

89

Write a song based on an old saying, platitude, homily, aphorism, e.g., his bark was worse than his bite. There are more fish in the sea. An ounce of prevention is worth a pound of cure.

90

Set a recipe to music.

91

Write a cowboy song. 1 5 6 1, 1 5 6 1 . . .

92

Write a kid's song to teach some subject matter, like the history of your state or the names of trees.

93

Write about an invention or an inventor or an explorer.

94

Play with line lengths that are very wordy—as in "Auctioneer" by LeRoy Van Dike and Buddy Black—or sparse—as in "Soul Deep" by Wayne Carson. Try to write one-word, two-word, three-word, and four-word phrases with lots of space around the words. Restrict yourself to only four-syllable lines, as in Hank Williams' "Your Cheatin' Heart."

95

Write a song haiku or set an existing haiku to music. For instance, "Moonlight in Vermont" (by John Blackburn and Karl Suessdorf) is a haiku.

96

Think of the most nasal song you can, and write in that voice.

97

Think of the most throaty or breathless song you can, and write in that voice.

98

Play with the confusion of sexuality and religion (the way some of Madonna's songs do). Write something irreverent or as reverent as you can make it, using either sex or religion as the main topic. Set out to shock or embarrass yourself.

99

Pick up an instrument you don't normally play and noodle a bit.

100

Make some sounds associated with repetitive gestures—like sewing, turning a waterwheel, hammering, chopping wood—and choreograph them.

101

Write about a vehicle (boat, car, plane, train, escalator).
Good examples are "If I had a Boat" and "Which Way Does That
Old Pony Run?" (both by Lyle Lovett).

102

Write a swing tune called "Mood Swing" (Lou Barlow and John Davis) or "The Swing Set" (Richard Bowles) or another pun that refers to a musical style or instrument in the title. For example, "When I Was Green, I Didn't Have the Blues" (Lisa Aschmann and Fred Koller) or "Sax Appeal" (Kim Waters). Write a song for a particular instrument that illustrates its range and timbre.

103

Write a mystery or ghost story, e.g., "Long Black Veil" by Danny Dill and Marijohn Wilkin.

104

Scatter five arbitrary nouns on a piece of paper down the page and then write in the spaces around them to fill in the meaning (like you do with Mad Libs).

105

Reverse syntax or the parts of speech. Make verbs act as nouns and nouns act as verbs or make adjectives nouns. For example, "Home" by Karla Bonoff.
"Home sings me of sweet things . . .
My life there has its own wings
Fly me over the mountain
Though I'm standing still . . . "

106

Use gerunds (present passive voice verbs), e.g., "Running With the Night" (Lionel Richie and Cynthia Weil) or "Flying Down to Rio" (Gus Kahn, Edward Eliscu, and Vincent Youmans).

107

Pick a meter and stick two or four bars of another meter in a section of the song, e.g., "Have a Heart" by Bonnie Hayes. Go out of step and insert extra notes or phrases in some places, deliberately crowding a line.

108

Use counter-rhythms or polyrhythms and write over them using a call-and-response form.

109

Establish a bass run that repeats and adds a counter-rhythm, e.g., "Lady Madonna" and "Blackbird" (Lennon and McCartney), "Liza (All the Clouds'll Roll)" (George Gershwin, Ira Gershwin, and Gus Kahn), "Fields of Gold" (Sting).

110

Write a song using an unusual rhythm, such as 3/2 or 5/8 time.

111

Make a song *about* rhythms, e.g., "I Like to Play in 7/8 Time" (Lisa Aschmann and Jamey Whiting).

112

Write a rap song.

113

Write a song using a Bo Diddley rhythmic motif, a Buddy Holly
motif, a Babyface motif (i.e., cop a feel).

114

Write a song about dancing, e.g., "I Could Have Danced All Night"
(Lerner and Loewe) or "You Make Me Feel Like Dancing"
(Leo Sayer and Vincent Poncia).

115

Write a jumprope skipping song. Examples: "In came the
doctor, in came the nurse, in came the lady with the
alligator purse . . . "; "Not last night but the night before,
twenty-four robbers came knockin' at my door . . . ";
"Salt, pepper, vinegar, and wine . . . "

116

Switch a "straight" groove to "swing" or vice versa.
Emphasize 8th notes and/or triplets in a rhythm. Use
straight 8's rock, a 12/8 ballad, or a 4/4 swing feel.
Use syncopation, e.g., rock ballad, swing feel. Louis Jordan
was a master at this type of changeover from straight to
swing and so was that other Louis, Louis Armstrong.

117

Think of as many sensual details as you can and cluster them
around a particular sense, such as smell or touch.

118

Write a song that doesn't rhyme anywhere.

119

Write a song that rhymes in groups of three and then has
one unrhymed word.

120

Meditate awhile. Write something that might get you
in the mood to do this.

121

Copy somebody else's song form exactly, using their melody
(write a parody), and then change the melody.

122

Here's a list of potential writing topics from
Elaine Farris Hughes' book, *Writing From the Inner Self:*
Sensuous pleasures
Future daydreams
Things I'm keeping from myself
Good things about my life
Ways I'm unkind to myself
Unusual experiences I have had
The masks I wear
Old yearnings
New ambitions
All the things that are okay about me
All the things I want
People I miss
Childhood delights
Some gratitudes
Why I'll never be (or *will* be) a writer
Feelings that cause me the most trouble
Objects I have loved
My favorite room
What I think about men (or women)
My favorite songs or artists (this ought to stoke you
like nothing else will; listen to some great songs!)

123

Write a song about being fat (or thin), about dieting or eating,
e.g., "Rolly Poley" ("daddy's little fatty") by Fred Rose or
"Big Boned Gal" by k.d. lang.

124

Write about body parts that have no sensations, e.g., "My hair and my fingernails don't give a shit about you" (comment by Bob Brozman).

125

Use as many five-syllable adverbs as you can in a lyric, e.g., "I'm speaking to you confidentially . . . "

126

Write a song using only one-syllable words.

127

Two blind people going at it with hammer and scissors: Write about violence from an amused perspective. Shel Silverstein has some outrageous ones: "The Winner" and "Three Legged Man" come to mind. Or, write about violence from a serious perspective. There are some great anti-war songs out there, but there can't be too many.

128

Think of things you do in fourth grade that stigmatize you for life.

129

Here we go again. Reflect on repetition, things that have happened over and over in history or in your personal relationships.

130

Write a song with only two chords. Examples: "Tulsa Time" (Danny Flowers: 1, 5), "Achy Breaky Heart" (Don von Tress: 1, 5), "Just My Imagination Running Away With Me" (Barrett Strong and Norman Whitfield: 1, 5). How about using a two-chord form other than 1, 5? Try one with only three chords.

131

Write the bass line first.

132

Write the drum part first.

133

Write a song to heal a relationship.

134

Think of something about love you could exaggerate, e.g., "Forever," "Until the stars go out," "Your love can move mountains," etc.

135

Write a graduation theme, a year's end party song, a let's-go-to-the-beach song.

136

Write a lullaby.

137

Jorge Luis Borges in his book, *On Writing*, quotes Oscar Wilde: "Were it not for the sonnet or other set forms of verse, we would all be at the mercy of genius." Well, I told you what I thought of genius! By the way, W.B. Yeats, Kipling, and Robert Service are particularly fertile fields of poetry for songwriters. They're some great poets who've motivated excellent melodies. Set a sonnet or other tightly fixed form of poetry to music. Personally, I have had songs inspired by the writings of Edwin Arlington Robinson, Mary Oliver, Robert Frost, Rumi, St. John of the Cross, Sara Teasdale, and May Sarton. Try a strict-form poem, a free-form poem. Set a poem to music.

138

Write a song that has a minor 7th in it, like ("there's a place for us") "Somewhere" (Stephen Sondheim and Leonard Bernstein).

139

Write a song that has a major 7th in it, e.g., the second line of Henry Mancini's "Moon River" (" . . . I'm crossing you in style . . . ").

140

Compose a still life. Think of a particular object or set of objects that have some significance in their grouping and presentation. What does it mean to "capture" a scene? Compose an auditory collage. Borrow musical elements in their entirety; cut and paste.

141

Good idea: whistling while you work. Bad idea: whistling while you eat. Write a song about an incident where "It seemed like a good idea at the time" applies.

142

Write a song from the underdog's perspective. Give voice to somebody usually disenfranchised. Write from the villain's perspective or the perspective of an unfamous sidekick, such as Tonto or Sancho Panza. Examples: *Grendel* by John Gardner, "Mata Hari" and "Cyrano Ballet" (both by John Gart), or "Billy the Kid" (one each by Burl Ives, Skitch Henderson, and Aaron Copeland).

143

Do you have wanderlust? Tell why or why not.

144

Is there something about you that nobody in your family understands? Now's your chance to set them straight in a song.

145

Start with an octave, e.g., "When You Wish Upon a Star" (Ned Washington and Leigh Harline) or "Somewhere Over the Rainbow" (E.Y. "Yip" Harburg and Harold Arlen).

146

Imagine how heroes, such as Zorro, Conan the Barbarian, Batman,
Amelia Earhart, Eleanor Roosevelt, Martin Luther King Jr., handle fear.
Use fear and conquering fear as a theme in your writing.

147

Meeting and overcoming obstacles is the central plot in most film scripts. And
guess what industry needs lots of music at those plot points?

148

Recall your first days of elementary school, junior high school, high school,
college; remember your first girlfriend/boyfriend, first job, first boss. What did
you tell yourself? What was terrible? What was great? Experience that fear
again. How do you cope?

149

You're at your parent's grave site. What do you say?

150

You're saying good-bye to your kid, driving him or her to college.
What do you say?

151

You're at your golden wedding anniversary party. What do you say?

152

You're trying to persuade your family to move to the country (or the city) from
where they are. Extol the virtues of the other place.

153

You gotta brag. Go ahead, tell the people what's so special
about you, him, her, us.

154

Testify about something you've learned. Warn somebody about the mistake they're going to make, e.g. "He Don't Love You Like I Love You" (Jerry Butler, Curtis Mayfield, and Carlton Carter), "Mamas, Don't Let Your Babies Grow Up to Be Cowboys" (Ed and Patsy Bruce).

155

You caught somebody in a lie; confront them in a song.

156

What's the song that would go best with a shimmy and sequins?

157

What's the song that would go best with a top hat and cane?
A smoky dive? A big ballroom?

158

What's the song that would go best with a ten gallon hat?

159

Write about an unusual way of life—for example, the lion tamer's song, the pipe fitter's song, the pastry chef's song; e.g., Jimmy Webb's "Wichita Lineman." Write about hoboes, street people, and the unemployed; and rather than just observe their blues, find something unexpected in them to write about.

160

Birds, flowers, rivers. Connect one of these to an emotion, e.g., "The Redtail Hawk" by Josh Graves or "River" by Bill Staines.

161

Write a song that an exercise class could work out to.

162

Put as many colors or as much color as you can into a lyric,
e.g., Prince's "Raspberry Beret."

163

You visited a gypsy/palmist/card reader. What did they say?

164

Write a song about a sport. Examples: "Golf Is a Four-letter Word," "This Is the
NFL" (Rolfe Wyer II and Peter Dergee), "Dropkick Me, Jesus" ("through the
goalposts of life") (Paul Craft).

165

What happened "Just in Time"
(Adolph Green, Jule Styne, and Betty Comden)?

166

Write a train song, that is, a song using a "train" rhythm, like
"My Baby Thinks He's a Train" by Leroy Preston.

167

Write a "cat on the keys" song and remember what they say about jazz:
"There are no wrong notes in jazz."

168

Create your own Dr. Seuss character and his/her/its song.

169

What would extinct animals (a dinosaur, a dodo bird) have to say about the
world as it is? What would a fictional character, such as Rip van Winkle, say?

170

Pretend you're a different age than you are and write in that voice,
e.g. "All I Want for Christmas Is My Two Front Teeth" (Don Gardner).

171

What is a good lover? Friend? Buddy? Who is a good lover? Friend? Buddy?
What are they like? What is a mensch? Who is a mensch to you?

172

Miracles never cease. Write about some everyday miracles or
some "Wonders of the World." Write about magic.

173

Make the distinction between a lady, a woman, and a girl and write about
them, or tell why they're the same in somebody.

174

Defend somebody who's been attacked.

175

Rewrite clichés, write from them, or write them into your song. Here are
some suggestions: out of the clear blue sky, pay dearly, alive and well, in no
time flat, down in the dumps, a complete disaster, my one and only, reckless
abandon, eyes glued, shivers up my spine, broke my heart, racked my brain,
heavy as a rock, quiet as a mouse, sharp as a tack, light as a feather, well
aware, last but not least, not a care in the world, a lump in my throat, safe
and sound, a rude awakening.

176

Take a song lyric that you've already written, draw a circle around each cliché,
then replace each cliché with an original lyric.

177

Write about the same-old-same-old. Are you bored or comforted by it? Use parallel construction to reveal repetition. For example: "Life Gits Tee'jus, Don't It?" by Carson Robison or "Every day, the sun, and after sunset, night, and her stars . . ." (Ralph Waldo Emerson).

178

Strip away some masks of adulthood; e.g., "Other people cannot see what I see. Whenever I look into your father's face, far behind your father's face as it is today are all those other faces which were his. Let him laugh and I see a cellar your father does not remember and a house he does not remember and I hear in his present laughter his laughter as a child" (James Baldwin).

179

Keep a journal for a week if you haven't already. A lifetime would be good.

180

Write about a party, for a party, having a party, a ceilidh, a rite of passage, a wake, something festive, or something that should be festive but isn't, e.g., "Mama Told Me Not to Come" (Randy Newman). Use the soundscape (e.g., William Carlos Williams on Bruegel's painting: "the squeal and the blare and the tweedle, the bugle and the fiddles, tipping their bellies").

181

Write the background music to a chase scene. (Fire engines and cars flying off the ends of piers optional.)

182

What have you been avoiding? Speak up. As in that Elton John and Bernie Taupin song "Your Song" or "I'll Have to Say I Love You in a Song" by Jim Croce, this may be your chance to say what otherwise might be hard to put into words. Let songwriting make telling *easier*.

183

Push "the little engine that could."

184

Gossip. Do a best/worst list, or tell how gossip has affected you, e.g.,
"I Heard It Through the Grapevine" (Norman Whitfield and Barrett Strong)
or "New Kid in Town" (Glenn Frey, Don Henley, and J.D. Souther).

185

Write down the rules of formulaic commercial songwriting as you know
them . . . then break them—BLAM!—one by one. Or parody them. For
example, "Blah Blah Blah" (George and Ira Gershwin) was written as a protest
against all the rhymes conventionally used for "moon." "Scrambled Eggs" was
the original title to Paul McCartney's "Yesterday." "Achy Breaky Heart" was
written after writer Don von Tress failed to get several serious, personal songs
published. Write the absolute most trite, stupid song you can, using the stuff
you hate the most. My personal hit list includes the rhymes "higher," "desire,"
and "fire." Also, I detest the phrase, "tore my heart in two."

186

Debunk some of the great laws through the ages: the world is flat, the sun
revolves around the earth, underwear has to be white, nice guys finish last,
your face will freeze in that position, all the good ones are taken . . .

187

Tell the history of a house or set the action in one of these rooms: bedroom,
parlor, sauna, hallway, kitchen, cellar, foyer, transept, boudoir, laboratory, den,
nook, attic, belfry. Back at the old corral? Back at the cave?

188

Take an article of clothing and make it emblematic of a person's experience.
Examples: "Hi Heel Sneakers" (Robert Higginbotham), "Blue Suede Shoes"
(Carl Perkins), "This Shirt" by Mary Chapin Carpenter.

189

Put a person and a flavor together, e.g., your lover and cinnamon, sassafras, ginger, apple, mango, butter. What was his/her cooking like? Where did you go and what did you eat on that picnic by the lake, after church, at the beach, at the drive-in.

190

Write a monster song for Halloween.

191

Write about a force of nature: He/she's a "Hurricane With Two Eyes" (Lisa Aschmann and Henry Hipkens); "Shake, Rattle, and Roll" by Charles Calhoun; or "I Feel the Earth Move" by Carole King.

192

Pay musical tribute to cartoon characters, e.g., Betty Boop, Ren and Stimpy, Scooby Doo, the seven dwarves, Daffy Duck, the Flintstones, Bullwinkle, Garfield, the Simpsons, Bugs Bunny, Snoopy.

193

Euro-pop or techno-pop music makes heavy use of synthesizers. Write something with as many samples or different synthesizer sounds as you can fit in. Write a symphony. Write a rock opera.

194

Write something for a great instrumentalist, living or dead, such as Jimi Hendrix or Liszt, to be challenged by.

195

Write the simplest song you could teach to a five-year-old.

196

Write a cheer.

197

Write an acronym.

198

Write a song for an unborn child.

199

Rewrite existing songs with one-third of the notes, then add different ones.

200

Write a song for doing laundry by hand. If you were washing clothes at the river, for instance, what would your song be?

201

What falls? Leaves fall. You fall asleep. You fall in love. What gives? What sways? What breaks? Group verbs that might emotionally key a song.

202

Flatter and pamper somebody verbally.

203

Write about energy and sex. Chemistry! Electricity! Wind me up. Pull my string. Big wind, cool wind, Niagara Falls, heat wave.

204

Write a song for a red letter day such as payday, getting out of jail, your class reunion, Sunday morning, Friday (TGIF), or Saturday night.

205

Write Muzak for the elevator, the roller coaster, the elephant parade, the cafeteria, the busboy, the pearl diver. If the beauty shop hair dryers had a song, what would it be? What about the five seconds of music that plays when you win a video game? Reward somebody with a little musical pat on the back.

206

Write another song for the Shakers or the Quakers or the Amish or the Luddites—people who like to keep it simple.

207

What would it mean to really serve someone? Do a mitzvah (good deed) in a song or *with* a song or talk about one in the lyrics.

208

Write down your dreams. They may contain juice for songs.

209

Write a song for each of the four directions: south, east, west, and north. Or write one song about all of them.

210

Write a chant for a ritual, e.g., a solstice celebration.

211

Games people play—what are they?

212

Comment on voices: a purr, a whine, a voice husky with emotion, a croak, a
sharp exhalation of breath, a deep honeyed voice, admonitory whispers,
uneasy laughter, quiet dignity, trembling with indignation. Or lilting,
quavering, cold, thin, reedy, prickling, savage, passionate, resonant, unsteady,
roaring, disembodied, tight, or triumphant tones.

213

Comment on smiles: a gentle smile, a tolerant smirk, an inviting smile, a flash
of curiosity, a grin. Try different gestures and illustrate them musically.

214

Write a march. Sousa is full of terrific examples (also Ives and Joplin).
You don't have to come down hard on the count of ONE two three four; you
could syncopate it. But then it might be a ragtime march.

215

Write a song about unlikely, but true, love. Think of two people at total
opposite ends of the social spectrum—e.g., the flower seller and the professor,
the schoolteacher and the king, rival gang members—and put them together
in a romantic duo. (This is the crux of most musical theater plots circa 1930-
50.) Write songs to introduce the characters and further the plot and you have
the beginnings of a musical. Maybe you'll want to pursue this.

216

Use a song to describe or define or affirm yourself, e.g., "That'll Be Me"
(Kevin Welch), "This Is Me" (Tom Shapiro and Thom McHugh),
"The Way I Am" (Sonny Throckmorton), etc.

217

Use the pace of a song to imitate the pace of sex or another event,
e.g., Ravel's "Bolero" imitates the buildup (or maybe Peter Gabriel's
"Sledgehammer" does).

218

A friend of mine, Jill Kramer, talks about the genre she calls "the sensitive rat" song, in which the main character sweetly justifies some obnoxious behavior (cheating, leaving, etc.). Some of the biggest sellers let 'em down easy. Try this out if you can't help yourself.

219

Write a song using a one-word title. For instance, "Faith" (Lisa Aschmann and Carol Hashe), "Physical" (Terry Shaddick and Stephen Kipner), "Anticipation" (Carly Simon), "Reunited" (Frederick Perren and Dino Fekaris), "Fame"(Dean Pitchford and Michael Gore), "Nagasaki" (Mort Dixon and Harry Warren).

220

Put some sequencing in your harmony, adding interior, and moving lines in the upper registers, e.g., Herman Hupfeld's "As Time Goes By." Or use a chained suspension, e.g., Jerome Kern's Em7→A7→Dmaj7 and Em9→A7$^{\#5}$→Dmaj9.

221

Feature a prominent chromatically descending bass line, like Henry Purcell's "Dido's Lament" or "Let It Be Me" by Manny Kurtz, Gilbert Silly, and Pierre Leroyer.

222

Feature a prominently ascending chromatic bass line, e.g., 1→#1dim→2→5.

223

Modulate like crazy. Examples: "Lover" by Richard Rodgers and Lorenz Hart, "The Song Is You" by Jerome Kern and Oscar Hammerstein or "I've Never Been in Love Before" by Frank Loesser.

224

Write a tango. Write a samba. Write a cueca.
Ever tried a cha cha? A merengue?

225

Use some ethnic, exotic instruments to sweeten up your tracks and inspire you
(e.g., the Turkish tzaz, the African mbira, the Japanese koto).

226

Put together a gamelan orchestra. How about a jug band?
Get out the spoons. Hambone.

227

Parody a vocal style. Imagine somebody you'd like to have record
your song and "target write" to their specifications. Put their voice,
what they're likely to say, and as much of their style as possible in
what you write. Some artists are particularly fun to imitate vocally
(e.g., Elvis, Dylan). How about Leon Redbone?

228

Write a song for different pavilions at the World's Fair, Expo, the Olympics,
etc. Does your team/town/state/country have a song yet?

229

Lead the ear to certain rhymes and then go someplace else
(e.g., "Nellie had a steamboat, the steamboat had a bell . . . ").

230

Rhyme in couplets only or use double and triple syllable rhymes
throughout a piece.

231

Use tons of inner rhymes. Cole Porter was a master: "Do do that voodoo that
you do so well" ("I've Got You Under My Skin").

232

Read the dedications, acknowledgments, and prefaces in books.
Who were these people to each other? You can get some vicarious pleasure out
of people expressing their gratitude and positive relationships to each other
(as well as a lot of choice song ideas). Autobiographies and books containing
letters are especially juicy for song ideas, particularly in the boyhood/girlhood
stages of people's lives.

233

If you play guitar, go up the neck, using chords that keep the
same basic shape of the fingers. Try different strums that you haven't
before. Try different tunings. DADGAD and G tunings may restrict your
choices, but they provide lots of open strings that could lead to nice
Celtic-inflected melodies and fiddle tunes.

234

Write music to accompany a contra dance or a square dance
complete with calls.

235

If you play banjo, write for different five-string or four-string frailing and
plucking techniques and compare them. Imitate an old-time American folk
style. If you play bass, try writing for fretted and fretless bass, standup bass,
bowed bass, or cello and compare them. If you play sax or recorder, play with
writing for the alto, tenor, and soprano versions of your instrument.
Experiment with instruments related to yours, e.g., dulcimer, hammered
dulcimer, autoharp, zither; accordion, concertina, squeezebox; organ, piano,
harpsichord, synthesizer.

236

Invent an "instrument" (e.g., comb and tissue paper, sticks, toilet paper rolls,
rattles). Write for a kazoo. Use a mouth harp or harmonica and see where it
takes you.

237

Write a subtractive song, which makes use of successively fewer and fewer words (e.g. "Little Rabbit in the Wood" or "Under the Spreading Chestnut Tree"). Or write a song that would be fun for a mime or a clown to perform silently.

238

Somebody reminds you of somebody else. Write about déjà vù or the way your memories play tricks on you.

239

Write about going fishing—e.g., "Baby's Goin' Fishin'," "Fishing Blues" (Henry Thomas and J.M. Williams) or "You and Me Goin' Fishin' in the Dark" (Wendy Waldman and Jim Photoglo), "Cruisin' " (Smokey Robinson), "Groovin' " (Felix Cavaliere and Eddie Brigati). Check out the scene at a bar or high school dance or the "Night Moves" (Bob Seger) afterward. Or hey, maybe just a song about fishing.

240

Use gambling metaphors, e.g., "The Joker" ("in the Deck") (Steve Miller), "I Feel Lucky" (Mary Chapin Carpenter and Don Schlitz), "Two of a Kind Workin' on a Full House" (Bobby Boyd, Warren Haynes, and Dennis Robbins), "Roll of the Dice" (Bruce Springsteen), "Aces" (Cheryl Wheeler), "Lily, Rosemary, and the Jack of Hearts" (Bob Dylan).

241

Where do you want to go when you die? Is there an afterlife? How do you want to be disposed of? Think about John Prine's "Please Don't Bury Me" or Tony Arata's "Someday I Will Lead the Parade."

242

What is perfect? Inviolate? Invincible? Sacred? True? "The best thing that ever happened to me . . . " etc. Use superlatives to describe something. Be fulsome with someone.

243

Understate the case, as in "(You're) Just a Little in Love"
(Ron Reynolds and Amanda Hunt).

244

Write a song that a modern dance troupe could choreograph, e.g.,
"Clockwork" (Alex de Grassi) or "On a Tightwire" (Steve Brown).

245

Write a song about a mythical beast—such as a gryphon, phoenix, or
unicorn—or mythology, like the stories "The Golden Fleece,"
"The Cyclops," and "Medusa."

246

The right thing to say. What was it? When?

247

What is the funniest thing you ever saw? Heard? The saddest?
The most beautiful?

248

How did your parents react to your boyfriend/girlfriend? How did your friends
react? To your breakup? To your engagement? What advice did they give?
(People are always chock full of advice.) Make something up if you can't
remember.

249

Write a song from the perspective of a person in circumstances far removed
from your own but with whom you can still identify—e.g., a Lapp, a Bedouin, a
wino, a nun, a Navajo, a geisha girl, a Southern sharecropper, a coal miner, an
organ grinder, a ventriloquist, a warden, an inmate, a pharaoh, a wandering
Jew (not a house plant!).

250

Ask a Socratic (leading) question that you know the answer to. Examples: "Do I Love You?" (Cole Porter), "Am I Blue?" (Grant Clarke and Harry Akst).

251

Change a reality premise slightly. For instance, "Twenty Five Hours a Day" (Craig Cooper), "Eight Days a Week" (Lennon and McCartney), "We'll have one hundred and twenty babies . . . " ("Anchorage" by Michelle Shocked).

252

State the obvious. Locate yourself. For example:
"Here I am" (Tony Arata), "I'm Not Lisa," ("my name is Julie")
(Jessi Colter), and "there you were" ("How Sweet It Is" by
Brian Holland and Lamont Dozier).

253

You wouldn't believe the number of songs that start with,
"Got up this morning" or "Sittin' here." Start with where you are.
Look around. Check in with yourself. How do you feel *right now?*
What's uppermost in your mind *right now?*

254

Write a zipper song. That's a song that "zips" a word or a line in and out of the rest of the existing structure. Examples: "She'll Be Comin' 'Round the Mountain," Si Kahn's "People Like You Help People Like Me Go On," or Holly Near's "Singing for Our Lives." Zipper songs are a good source of singalongs.

255

Write an additive song, e.g., "There's a Hole in the Bottom of the Sea," "The Ladies of the Court of King Koracticus," "Whoever Shall Have Some Good Peanuts" (Cathy Fink). These are songs that tell a story serially, by adding one element at a time, summing up the action in ever-longer choruses.

256

Write a riddle song, e.g., "I Gave My Love a Cherry," "Tumbalalaika," "There Were Three Sisters." Or write in a question/answer format, e.g., "There's a Hole in My Bucket" or "Can You Count the Stars?" (Jonathan Willcocks).

257

What makes you crazy? How are you crazy?

258

Wallow.

259

Bust out.

260

You rascal, you!

261

Give yourself a good talking to.

262

Write about the radio ("Turn Your Radio On" by Albert Brumley or "I'm a Radio" by Joni Mitchell), or the TV, or the news ("Dirty Laundry" by Don Henley).

263

Write for a barbershop quartet.

264

Write a madrigal. Write for a choir.

265

Write a song for three voices. Stacked bluegrass harmonies. A duet.

266

Set to music some instructions or "found poetry"; e.g., the Miranda rights, the stuff they tell you on airplanes about your oxygen mask in the overhead compartment, how to assemble a kid's toy, etc.

267

Go through Bartlett's *Familiar Quotations* or another compendium of quotable quotes and substitute "love" or "heart" for some of the other nouns. Rewrite familiar sayings or other people's song titles. For instance, "Somewhere Under the Rainbow" (Jerry Laseter, Kerry Phillips, and Scott Blackwell). Turn a phrase, e.g., "Home Is Where the Heart Aches" (Lisa Aschmann, Joel Evans, and J.D. Smith) or "The High Cost of Loving" (Hal Bynum and Dave Kirby).

268

Just for the pun of it, put some puns in your song; e.g., "I'd rather have a bottle in front of me than a frontal lobotomy" (W.C. Fields), "If I Said You Had a Beautiful Body" ("would you hold it against me?") (David Bellamy). And here's a verse I love from "The Swimming Song" by Loudon Wainwright III:
"This summer, I swam in a public place
And in a reservoir, to boot.
At the latter, I was informal.
At the former, I wore my suit."

269

Tell about what's possible in your relationship, e.g., "I Will" (Paul McCartney), "We Could" (Felice Bryant) or "Someday We'll Be Together" (Jackey Beavers and Johnny Bristol). Optimism in itself is a great theme in songwriting, e.g., "Rose Colored Glasses" (John Conlee and George Baber), "I Can See Clearly Now" (Johnny Nash).

270

Write about a disaster. Examples: "The Springhill Mine Disaster" (Peggy Seeger), "The Titanic" (Leadbelly), "Barrett's Privateers" (Stan Rogers), "The Wreck of the Old 97" (Fred Lewey, Charles Noell, and Henry Work), "The Wreck on the Highway" (Roy Acuff), "The Wreck of the Edmund Fitzgerald" (Gordon Lightfoot).

271

Write about a deal with the devil—e.g. "The Devil Went Down to Georgia" (Charlie Daniels) or "Shoeless Joe from Hannibal, Mo." (Jerry Ross and Richard Adler)—or pick another classic folktale to retell in song. What happened to Paul Bunyan and Pecos Bill? Coyote? Silke? Loki? Anansi?

272

Modernize a hero. For example, "Joe Hill" (Earl Robinson and Alfred Hayes) and "Geronimo's Cadillac" (Charles John Quarto and Michael Martin Murphy).

273

Write a "before you"/"after you" scenario; e.g., ("there were birds all around, but I never heard them singing,") "Till There Was You" (Meredith Willson) or ("you made me leave my happy home; you took my love and now you're gone . . . ") "Since I Fell for You" (Buddy Johnson). People change, sometimes everything, for each other.

274

Have you ever written a rockabilly tune? Everybody thinks of Elvis, but how about Carl Perkins, Jerry Lee Lewis, or Gene Vincent?

275

How about a conjunto tune, or a Tex-Mex tune?

276

Start the chorus right *on* the downbeat, e.g., "Blue Skies" ("smiling at me . . .") (Irving Berlin), "Roll Out the Barrel" (Vaclav Zeman, Jaromir Vejvoda, Wladimir Timm, and Lew Brown).

277

Look up movies in production in *The Hollywood Reporter* or a similar trade magazine and see if you can get in on the ground floor by writing something appropriate for them; something somebody's working on may not have the music yet. Or write what ought to be the sequel to existing shows and themes, the trailer music, etc.

278

Make a long story short.

279

Make a list of dos and don'ts:
"Don't Fence Me In" (Cole Porter)
"Don't Let Your Deal Go Down"
"Ruby, Don't Take Your Love to Town" (Mel Tillis)
"Don't Be Cruel" (Otis Blackwell)
"Love Me Like You Used To" (Paul Davis and Bobby Emmons)
"Mind Your Own Business" (Hank Williams)
"Move It on Over" (Hank Williams)
"Act Naturally" (Voni Morrison and Johnny Russell)
"Build Me Up" (John Colla and Hugh Cregg)
"Do That to Me One More Time" (Toni Tennille)
"Run to Me" (Barry, Maurice, and Robin Gibb)

280

Put a stop or sudden rest in a rhythm. Use a vocal that's not singing—e.g., "Pretty Woman" when Roy Orbison growls or the "Ahoo! Ahoo!" in "Werewolves of London" (Warren Zevon). Or talk part of your melody, e.g., "Take This Job and Shove It" (David Allan Coe) or "Ragtime Cowboy Joe" (Lewis Muir and Hubert Arnold).

281

Write new melodies over these strong progressions:
$$1 \rightarrow 5 \rightarrow 1,$$
$$1 \rightarrow 6^{min} \rightarrow 2^{min} \rightarrow 5 \rightarrow 1,$$
$$1 \rightarrow 3^{min} \rightarrow 6^{min} \rightarrow 2^{min} \rightarrow 5 \rightarrow 1$$

282

Write about being young, e.g., "Young Blood" (Jerry Leiber, Doc Pomus, and Mike Stoller) or "young hearts, be free tonight" ("Young Turks" by Rod Stewart). Does the future beckon to you? Maybe you're "Forever Young" (Bob Dylan).

283

Write a song with "yes," "no," or "maybe" in the title.

284

Go for the absolutes. Finish these phrases:

I never _____.
I only _____.
I always _____.
I'm gonna _____.
I still _____.
Everything_____.
Nothing_____.

285

J'accuse. Start with "you." Examples: "You" (Tom Snow), "You Ain't Seen Nothin' Yet" (Randy Bachman), "You Don't Have to Be a Baby to Cry" (Bob Merrill and Terry Shand), "You Can't Hurry Love" (Eddie Holland, Lamont Dozier, and Brian Holland), "You Are the Sunshine of My Life" (Stevie Wonder). As you can see, starting like this can give rise to either a really intimate or really general, universal lyric.

286

Write about money, affluence, or lack of same. Philosophize.
Is it everything? Is it nothing? How much does it matter? For instance,
"Big Spender" (Dorothy Fields and Cy Coleman), "Forever in Blue Jeans" (Neil
Diamond and Richard Bennett), "Flower Lady" (Phil Ochs),
"Pocket Full of Gold" (Vince Gill).

287

Go to the movies. John Hartford tells the story of having written
"Gentle on My Mind"—the most often played song in America—after
having seen *Dr. Zhivago.*

288

Write a song somebody could do a hula to. Write with Hawaiian guitar or pedal
steel in mind. How about steel drums?

289

Write a song using Dobro or sympathetic strings added, a slide on the guitar,
or some other specialty attachment to an instrument.

290

Write a song about "one" of something. Examples: "One Trick Pony"
(Paul Simon), "One Mint Julep" (Rudolph Toombs), "One More Try" (Bobby
Gene Hall, Jr. and Raymond Simpson), "One Tin Soldier" (Dennis Lambert
and Brian Potter), "One of These Nights" (Don Henley and Glenn Frey), "You
Are the One" (Carroll Carroll and John Scott Trotter). Write about how
somebody or something is unique. Write about how somebody or something is
"just one more" in a line or a bunch.

291

Make up a dance and a song to go with it. "Mashed Potatoes,"
"The Watusi," "The Twist," and "Cotton-Eyed Joe" were once just a gleam in
some songwriter's eye. And what about "Walk Like an Egyptian" (Liam
Sternberg), "Loco-motion" (Carole King and Gerry Goffin), "And they'll be
dancin' . . . dancin' in Chicago . . . down in New Orleans . . . " (from "Dancing
in the Street" by Marvin Gaye, William Stevenson,
and Ivy George Hunter).

292

What did you two lovebirds fight about? Aren't you sorry now?

293

A lifetime of longing. If only . . . If you had it to do over . . .
Promises. Fulfilled. Unfulfilled. Explore your regrets.
But for godsakes, don't stay there!

294

Flagellate yourself. Hey, it was good enough for the plague years.
Crawl a little. For instance, ("I'll be") "Working My Way Back to You"
(Sandy Linzer and Denny Randell), ("I'd get") "Down on My Knees"
(Beth Nielsen Chapman), "Guilty" (Randy Newman),
"Sorry Seems to Be the Hardest Word" (Elton John).

295

Speak for more than yourself; use first person plural; e.g., "We Are the World"
(Lionel Richie and Michael Jackson), "We Belong" (Eric Lowen and Dan
Navarro), "We Shall Overcome," "We Can Work It Out" (John Lennon and
Paul McCartney), "We Will Rock You" (Brian May). Get big and anthemic, e.g.,
"Un Mundo" by Stephen Stills.

296

Use the telephone as a lyrical device. For instance, "Operator" was a title used by the Grateful Dead, the Manhattan Transfer, and Jim Croce, to name a few. Lately there have been lots of telephone answering machine songs, and there's even a musical called *Bells Are Ringing* (Jule Styne, Adolph Green, and Betty Comden). When will faxes and e-mail start cropping up in lyrics? Or how about doorbells? Doors? Windows? Fences? Gates? The postal service? Maybe you have some feelings associated with them.

297

Ask for help in a song—"Help" (Lennon and McCartney), "Help Me" (Joni Mitchell), "Help Me Make It Through the Night" (Kris Kristofferson), "Help Me, Rhonda" (Mike Love and Brian Wilson)—or offer it—"Help Is on the Way" (Robert Hunter and Jerry Garcia)—or just talk about that feeling—"Helpless" (Neil Young), "Helpless Heart" (Paul Brady), "I Need You to Turn To" (Elton John and Bernie Taupin).

298

What will never change, no matter what?

299

Pick a number. A popular one to write about is the number two, e.g., "Two Doors Down" (Dolly Parton), "Two Sides" (Scott Davis), "Two Hearts" (Bruce Springsteen), "Two Out of Three Ain't Bad" (Jim Steinman). If you are part of a dyad, you could write about "Us" (Burt Bacharach and Bobby Russell) or "Our House" (Graham Nash), etc. Does the number two make you feel divided and schizophrenic or cozy and comfortable in your relationship?

300

Use "so" or "very" or "all" in a song title. Get emphatic.

301

Use the diminutive, e.g., "Little . . . " "Baby . . . " "Honey . . . " "Darlin' . . . " "Sugar . . . " "Child . . . " Ooh! What a way to address somebody!

302

Question reality; e.g., "Can This Be Real?" (Janice Huston, Lee Hutson, and Michael Hawkins), "This Can't Be Love" (Rodgers and Hart). Question your dream; e.g., "Do I Love You Because You're Beautiful?" ("or are you beautiful because I love you?") (Rodgers and Hammerstein). Tackle the topic of imagination itself, e.g., "Impossible" from the musical *Cinderella* (also by Rodgers and Hammerstein): "And because these daft and dewy-eyed dopes keep building up impossible hopes, impossible things are happening every day." My sentiments *exactly!*

303

Ask why or where or what. When you're at your wits end, admit it. When you're lonesome, admit it. Songs are great vehicles for this kind of soul searching.

304

Marvel. "What a Wonderful World!" (Sam Cooke, Herb Alpert, Lou Adler), "Thank God I'm a Country Boy!" (John Martin Sommers).

305

Illness and infatuation have often been compared. Complain about your ailments. Do you have a "Fever" (John Davenport and Eddie Cooley)? A "Lovebug" (Curtis Wayne and Wayne Kemp)?

306

Notice how the grass is always greener? Write about envy, greed, invidious comparisons, e.g., "Jesse's Girl" (Rick Springfield), "What's He Got That I Ain't Got?" (Peter McCann), ("how come we're") "Always Looking?" (Roger Fennings, Charles Herndon, and Chip Raines), "Mom Always Liked You Best" (Thomas Smothers).

307

Persuade somebody to go to bed with you. No! No! In a *song*, silly!

308

Write a song that has a large descending interval at the beginning
of the chorus and then goes back up, e.g., Crowded House's ("Hey now,
hey now,") "Don't Dream It's Over" (Neil Finn) or Peter Cetera's
"Next Time I Fall" ("in love").

309

Write a song that has some sixteenth notes in it.
How about some four-count rests? A fermata?

310

Play with waltz time. Try writing one of each:
Viennese (a big downbeat on 1)
Cajun (emphasizing all 3 beats)
Jazz waltz (pushing beat 2 early)

311

Bless your heart, have you written your saint's day songs yet? St. Valentine's
Day? St. Nick's? How about St. Swithin's Day? And it's only fair to mention the
patron saint of travelers when you're traveling. How about mentioning St.
Peter at the Pearly Gates? Uh . . . St. James' infirmary?

312

The things we do for love! Write about something you'd roll your eyes or shake
your head about if you were older and wiser.

313

The two manmade items visible from space, so say the astronauts, are the
pyramids and the Great Wall of China. Suppose *you* were to write and make a
huge, lasting impression. Strive to make something "stick out" in the auditory
landscape, *way* out.

314

Write a song that goes outside the range of your own singing voice.

315

Write a song regarding wrestling.

316

Write a song of exultation, a breakthrough, a quest succeeding, a triumphant return.

317

Finish this phrase: Isn't it ironic that _____.

318

She's/he's hysterical. ("She's a") "Maniac" (Michael Sembello), "Jammed up and jelly tight" ("Blinded by the Light" by Bruce Springsteen), a monster, a "Wild Thing" (Chip Taylor), (Barney Jekyll and) "Bubba Hyde" (Craig Wiseman and Gene Nelson). What is the thing this person has turned into and why? On the dance floor? At a party? In bed? When they take off their shoes? When they put on their "Dancin' Shoes" (Carl Storie), does "Baby Like to Rock It" like the Tractors? Or what?

319

Try doo wop style. That is, write a triplet rhythm, drag on the count of 1, backbeat on 2 and 4: ONE and two and three and ONE. Examples: "This Boy" (Lennon and McCartney), "Tell It Like It Is" (George Davis and Lee Diamond), "Earth Angel" (Curtis Williams, Gaynel Hodge, and Jesse Belvin).

320

Play variations on 1 6 2 5 1, with passing tones. In the key of C, for instance: C Am Dm G C → C Cmaj7 Amin9 Dm$^{\#11}$ G$^{\flat9}$ Cmaj9. In other words, fancy up your chords.

321

Write on cultures in conflict/contact, e.g., "Ebony and Ivory" (Paul McCartney), "A Midnight Girl in a Sunset Town" (Don Schlitz), "All I Want to Be Is Understood" (Michael O'Hara, Denise Rich, and Mary Unobsky).

322

"When you're down and troubled, and you need a helping hand . . . " Console somebody. "You've Got a Friend" by Carole King is a good example of this type of song.

323

Yeah . . . serenity . . . I got your serenity right here, buddy. Write a song that shows 'em just how ticked off you are. Or comment on a song that's already out there that makes you mad; e.g., "God Didn't Make Honky Tonk Angels" (Jay Miller), "I Wish I Had a Job to Shove" (Billy Ray Reynolds and Ronnie Rogers).

324

Rue your hangover in a song—e.g., "Wasn't That a Party?" (Tom Paxton), "Too Much Tequila" (Dave Burgess)—or write about a party going awry—("we've been invited to") "Henrietta's Wedding" ("we can't tell when or where it will be . . . ") (Josef Marais and Gideon Fagan).

325

Write about the aging or physical imperfection of somebody as if it's unrelated to who they are as a person, e.g., "I'm a Little Cookie" (Larry Penn), "Walking on My Wheels" (Mark Cohen), "Forever and Ever, Amen" (Paul Overstreet and Don Schlitz).

326

Use the concept of shadows and light in a lyric. Clouds. Smoke. Fog. Candles.

327

Use some diminished chords. Get "spooky."

328

Use some augmented chords. Get "churchy."

329

Write a song for the child in your life. The child inside of you. Uh, the teenager with raging hormones?

330

Write a song for or on marimba, vibes, xylophone, or a related instrument. Play with a fork on glasses filled with various amounts of water. (If you have crystal goblets, so much the better. Lucky you!)

331

What did/do people tell you for your own good? Did/do you listen?

332

"Truckin'." If there's a profession that can use some accompanying music, that's got to be one of them, for example, "Drivin' My Life Away" (Eddie Rabbitt).

333

Write some muddy-sounding tracks for a garage band or grunge rock, etc. Feature lead guitar to the *hilt*.

334

Write a talking blues, like Woody Guthrie's "Dust Bowl Blues."

335

A corny song wouldn't be so bad, now, would it? It would just be . . . well . . . corny.

336

Take the highest note in your piece and ramp up to it and away from it. Build a mountain in the dead center of your piece.

337

Okay, okay, it's the moon's turn.
(Nobody's ever written about the moon, have they?)

338

Write a Christmas/Chanukah/winter solstice song. Write a carol.

339

Write about an ecology issue; teach kids about recycling, etc. Examples: Robert Palmer added new verses to Marvin Gaye's "What's Going On?" Mannheim Steamroller's soundtrack *Saving the Wildlife* is about whales, lions, pandas, penguins, etc. No dearth of concerns or topics here: acid rain, rain forest logging, etc. Some records are devoted to this topic, like Bill Oliver's album entitled "Don't Leave the Water Running When You Wash the Dog."

340

Take some historical scenario that moves you and explore what it must have been like, e.g., "The Journals of Susannah Moody" by Margaret Atwood or "Solitary Hero" by Carol Elliott and Alice Randall.

341

Sick, very sick. What does your sick sense of humor tell you? Maybe Weird Al Yankovic or Tom Lehrer lurks inside you. (Ray Stevens? Martin Mull?) Thank God for sick minds!

342

Lower the limbo stick. (Make the game harder for yourself. Up the ante.)

343

Think about a topic and cluster vocabulary around it. For example, regarding the parts of a castle, we have: the *bailey* (courtyard) walls, the *keep* (main house), the *great hall* (main room in the main house), the *drawbridge* over the moat, *parapets* (low walls along the top), *corbels* (stone brackets supporting the parapets), *machiolations* (holes in the parapets), *barbican* (forward gate before the *portcullis* or main gate), *postern* (back gate), *armory*, *gatehouse*, etc. Now you're closer to writing a song titled "A Man's Home" (Sheldon Harnick), "Castles in the Air" (Don McLean), "Castles in Spain," or "King of My Heart." Now, admittedly, some of these words don't sing very well. But if you get into most any topic, there will be specialized vocabulary to give you good, detailed pictures of it. Some of these more exact words will be the very thing to spice up your song. So, since we've got this list, how about it? Write a song about the king or princess or how defended somebody or something is, or how distant, or how fairy tale, or how grand.

344

Write a spiritually relevant story.

345

As Joseph Campbell said, "Follow your bliss." What else is there? Tell about your bliss. Has it always been this way?

346

Write about the passage of time. What are you *certain* of?

347

Finish these:

I'm not one to preach, but_____.
You've got to_____.
If you just _____.
All you have to do is _____.

348

What would you take to a desert island? And who?

349

Finish this thought: When you opened the door _____.

350

Write guidelines for kissing frogs or getting out of the swamp.

351

There is no place you need to be going to right now. You're home. Think about the experience, even if it just means connecting to the ownership of your own body and your own life.

352

Finish this phrase: If I had the power I'd _____.

353

You're losing control. How does it feel?
You're surrendering.
How does it feel?

354

Write a song for the massage table or the hot tub. Here are some examples to get you started: "Tenkuu" and "Silk Road" (both by Kitaro), "Dancing With the Lion" (Andreas Vollenweider), *Concert for the Earth* (Paul Winter), "Ancient Echoes" (Steve Halpern and Georgia Kelly), *Spectrum Suite* (Steve Halpern), "Birds of Paradise" and "Seapeace" (both by Georgia Kelly), *Poets and Angels* and *Nouveau Flamenco* (both by Ottmar Liebert).

355

Think about how you met him/her. Paint a picture, recapture the moment. Did you decide something or did it happen *to* you? Choices. Destiny. What *is* it? Example: "It Had to Be You" (Gus Kahn and Isham Jones).

356

Essential. Desirable. What's the difference? Or are they the same thing? What are you looking for that you must have, can't live without, etc.? What do you consider a luxury?

357

Using parallel 2nds or 4ths, make an oriental-sounding melody.

358

Ask a good question, like "How will I know?"

359

Take a title by a classical composer, such as Nocturne in E-flat (Chopin), Mass in C Minor (Mozart), Toccata and Fugue in D (Bach). They accomplish something in a certain key for that composer. Get into that key and try to let the very same title bring you to a different conception of the music that goes with it. A little night music? No problem! Name a key.

360

Go bananas. Milkshake. "Coconut" (as in "you put the lime in the . . . ") (Harry Nilsson). Write about food. My personal favorites are songs about potatoes.

361

Rouse us, e.g., Mongo Santa Marie and his African-Cuban band. Use bagpipes, tin whistles, trumpets. Do your own version of reveille. What gets you going in the morning besides coffee?

362

Write naked. That's right, starkers. In the buff. Sing in the shower, too.

363

Get dirty. Here are some suggestions: Go down to the river or turn the hose on some dirt. Make mud pies. Mud wrestle. Fingerpaint. What does this have to do with songwriting? Well, everything. Everything to do with getting in touch with your playful, childlike self. Break loose. Have fun, that's what.

364

Practice putting the hook in different places in your chorus. Write a doughnut. A doughnut has the hook in the first and last lines of the chorus. This is very common in Nashville writing. Examples: Wayland Holyfield and Bob House's "Could I Have This Dance" ("for the rest of my life")? or Bob Regan and Casey Kelly's "Soon." In a four-line chorus, try the following: Give lines 1 and 3 the same hook; 2 and 4 have different lines; e.g., "The Way It Is" by Bruce Hornsby. Or keep the hook in the first half of each line: "Fame" (Dean Pitchford and Michael Gore) or "She's Gone" (Daryl Hall and John Oates).

365

Pick up your dirty socks and put them in the hamper. Throw away that empty pizza box. If I sound like a mother, well, I am one; but that's not the point. Sometimes your creativity is blocked by clutter. If you create a little order around you before you begin, you might be pleasantly surprised. Do some obsessive thing, like sharpen all your pencils and line them up in order of size. Study which one has the most lead or which one is the sharpest. By all means, use your *favorite* one!

366

Imagine you're 16. Imagine you're 45. Imagine you're 101.
Oy! Imagine you're 2.

367

Artist's autobiographies, besides being generally inspiring, have cool titles with great advice in them. For example: Etta James' *Rage to Survive*, Sammy Davis Jr.'s *Yes I Can*, Shirley MacLaine's *Out On a Limb* and *Dancing in the Light*. Or Richard Feynman's two-volume autobiography, *Surely You're Joking, Mr. Feynman* and *What Do You Care What Other People Think?*

368

Think like a cloud. You are a cloud.

369

I want to write a national anthem for grizzly bears. The color purple, the planet Xenon, and my navel are things I constantly think about. I wear a spaghetti colander on my head when I'm in this mood. I go to the laundromat in my zirconium hat . . . and . . . receive . . . signals . . . Get it? Act weird. It isn't acting if you are—weird.

370

Vanilla? You don't know from vanilla.

371

If you haven't written lyrics first and melody second, do that. If you haven't written melody first and lyrics second, do that. Do the opposite of your normal writing process.

372

"9 to 5" (Dolly Parton), "Nightshift" (Walter Orange and Dennis Lambert), "She Works Hard for the Money" (Donna Summers), "Living for the City" (Stevie Wonder), "Morning Train (Nine to Five)" (Sheena Easton), "Car Wash" (Norman Whitfield) . . . You get the idea. Let your work work for you. Sure, gripe about it. Why not? You're not on company time.

373

Use the command form and make it active in a title: "Jump!" (Curtis Mayfield or Van Halen), "Shout!" (Isley Brothers).

374

Play dress up. Boots. Feather Boa. Epaulettes. Shades.

375

Whine. Beg. Plead for mercy. Cajole. Con. Examples: "Good Mornin',
Judge . . . " (Wynonie Harris), "Officer Krupke" (Leonard Bernstein),
"Sarge, I'm only eighteen . . . " ("Draft Dodger Rag" by Phil Ochs).

376

Assure somebody of your friendship, e.g., "That's What Friends Are For"
(Burt Bacharach and Carole Bayer Sager). ("You can count on me")
"Count on My Love" (Jesse Barish).

377

Assure somebody of your loyalty and devotion, e.g., "You Are Every Woman in
the World to Me" (Dominic King and Frank Musker), "I Only Have Eyes for
You" (Harry Warren and Al Dubin).

378

Get coy. "Do You Think I'm Sexy?" (Rod Stewart),
("it's the") "Right Time of the Night" (Peter McCann).

379

Probe your motivations. To get paid? To get laid? To show off? To praise God?
To make 'em dance. To make 'em cry. To exorcise some demons. To shed
some light. Find out more about your intentions. They'll crop up in your
music anyhow, guaranteed.

380

Focus on a single disturbing or wonderful world event, e.g., "The Night They
Drove Old Dixie Down" (Robbie Robertson), "The Night Chicago Died"
(Lionel Stitcher and Pete Callander). To refresh your memory, here are some
shockers: Tienanmen Square; the collapse of the Berlin Wall; the Exxon *Valdez*;
the shoot-out in Waco, Texas; the Oklahoma City bombing; the unibomber;
the exodus from Albania; the Trail of Tears.

381

Write a biography for a real person, e.g., "Vincent" (by Don McLean) about Vincent van Gogh or "Candle in the Wind" (by Elton John) about Marilyn Monroe.

382

Here's a plot: Friends turn into lovers, e.g., "Friends and Lovers" by Paul Gordon and Jay Gruska. Here's another plot: Lovers turn into friends, e.g., "I Will Always Love You" by Dolly Parton.

383

"Tonight, I Celebrate My Love for You" (Michael Masser and Gerry Goffin). Find a way to do this in a song.

384

Write a biography for an imaginary person, e.g., "Eleanor Rigby" (Lennon and McCartney).

385

"Honey" (Bobby Goldsboro), "Shake, Sugaree" (Elizabeth Cotton), "Sugartime" (Charlie Phillips and Odis Echols, Jr.), "Sugar, Sugar" (Jeff Barry and Andy Kim), "Sugartown" (Lee Hazelwood), "Sweet Magnolia Blossom" (Billy Crash Craddock), "My Sweet Lord" (George Harrison). Get the picture? It's gotta be *sweet* to spend time with that person.

386

Play with the spelling of a word, e.g., "There's No 'U' in Tennessee," "The Last Word in Jesus Is 'Us.' "

387

Write a song that's in a minor key in the verse, major in the chorus. Then write a song that's in a major key in the verse, minor in the chorus.

388

Play with "harmonic rhythm" (i.e., how fast the chords change in your song). Don't have chords always changing at the same rate. Varying this element doesn't need to affect the overall rhythmic structure.

389

Ever write Dixieland music? Big band style (a thirty-two bar intro, sixteen-bar verses, and a sixteen or thirty-two bar chorus)? How about a piano rag? It's fun to imitate vintage styles. How about a crooner? A torch-style ballad?

390

Take different "thin sections" of a setting. Tell about the thinnest sliver of time. Have your story take place in a split second. Over a lifetime. Over generations. Over eons.

391

Men! Women! Can't live with 'em, can't live without 'em. Duke it out with the opposite sex in a lyric. How are they so different? Or are they? How do you know/enjoy/resent your gender? What are some things you do on a regular basis that are typically masculine/feminine? What are some things you do on a regular basis that are atypical of your gender?

392

Dry. Cool. Wet. Soft. Thorny. Play with textures and sounds together. Have you got synesthesia? Do you hear colors? Fabrics?

393

Write a ballet for kids. Examples: *Peter and the Wolf* (Sergei Prokofiev), *The Nutcracker* (Peter Tchaikovsky), *Hansel and Gretel* (Engelbert Humperdinck), *Sleeping Beauty* (Igor Stravinsky and Peter Tchaikovsky). How about a ballet of *E.T., Star Wars, Indiana Jones*, or some other popular kid's story? How about music for ice skating tournaments or gymnastics routines?

394

Some famous composers left unfinished work. For instance, Symphony No. 8 in B Minor by Franz Schubert was never finished. Maybe you could write the next movement for him.

395

Regarding the pulse of music: People walk about two steps per second. A brisk walk is about 130 steps per minute, and 110 steps per minute is ambling. Feel how music at your walking tempo, your breathing rhythm, and your varying heart rate can be used to express (or manipulate) emotion. There's a story that Pete Townshend of The Who, while kicking his heroin habit, used a strobe light to stimulate his brain waves to desired, endorphin-releasing frequencies. Then he wrote the introduction to "Won't Get Fooled Again" to the same pulse as his strobe.

396

Try writing with a stop watch or minute minder. Race yourself. Do stream of consciousness writing in five-minute bursts. Write with a set duration in mind, the way jingle writers do. Write a thirty-second spot, a sixty-second spot, or a song that clocks in at exactly three minutes.

397

Tap something. Cause something to vibrate. Here are some things to drum on: pots and pans, garbage can lids, plastic buckets, empty jars and bottles, fence posts, screens, grates, anything corrugated, stop signs, umbrellas, lampshades, steel bridges, suspension cables, lamp posts, awnings, tents, walls, doors, windows. I got most of this list from W.A. Mathieu, but I find, in my own life, that spoons, toothbrushes and drinking glasses, coffee cans, and slapping my lap are my drum choices . . . Oh, and the shower head microphone . . . Ever try just making mouth noises? Pops, clicks, whistles. Underwater gargling. (Hey, Handel isn't the only one who writes "water music"!) Singing into a toilet paper roll is using an inexpensive reverb unit; an empty water cooler jug makes a mighty fine delay unit, too. Ever tried pantyhose/coat hanger microphone screens? See? The tools of your trade are *everywhere.*

398

What music should they play at your graduation? Your bar mitzvah? Your confirmation? Your induction? Uh . . . your coronation? Do you require, like Tchaikovsky's "1812 Overture" over "La Marseillaise," a few discreet cannons?

399

Say "please" (it's the magic word, isn't it?) and "thank you," e.g., "Baby, Please Don't Go" (Big Joe Williams), "Please Stay" (Burt Bacharach and Bob Hilliard), "Please Send Me Someone to Love" (Percy Mayfield), "Please, Please Me" (Lennon and McCartney), "Please, Mr. Postman" (Brian Holland, Robert Bateman, and Freddie Gorman).

400

"I Told You So" (David Sanborn and Hiram Bullock); "I Told You Once" (Jerry Irby). I *told* you. So, what is it again that we can't get through our thick skulls? Do tell.

401

Make fun of a dialect, e.g., "Josephine, Please No Lean on the Bell" (Ed Nelson, Harry Pease, and Robert Leonard) popularized by Eddie Cantor in the "roaring" forties.

402

If you're going to be down in a song, take us *way* down, e.g., Doug Stone's "I'd Be Better Off (In a Pine Box)"; Randy Newman's "I Think It's Going to Rain Today." Many writers owe Leonard Cohen a lot of gratitude for showing them where their veins are located.

403

Landmarks . . . In the year I was born . . . What happened? Find out. Or find out who else had a birthday and write about them. For example, Cheryl Wheeler has a song about the year that the Yellow Cab Company was founded. Mary Chapin Carpenter has a song about Haley's comet.

404

Finish this phrase: Ain't nothin' wrong with me that a little _____ won't cure. (What about snake oil, lovin' . . .)

405

In an otherwise 1 4 5 tune, try this traditional but cool progression: $1{\rightarrow}4^{\flat\,7}{\rightarrow}5$ as in "Salt Creek," "Red Haired Boy," and "Old Joe Clark."

406

Start your song going up a major sixth—"My Bonny Lies Over the Ocean"—or going down a major sixth—"Nobody Knows the Trouble I've Seen." Try descending with a major third, e.g., "Swing Low, Sweet Chariot." Get big and brave with the starts you make.

407

A.J. and Sean Breen told me that this idea was Brian Eno's: Get three envelopes and several index cards. On each envelope, write either "style," "key," or "theme." Then write ideas on the cards that fall under these categories. Put the appropriate cards into each envelope. Draw one card from each envelope and write the resulting combination. Or keep a card file and pull out one of these cards at random.

408

Do whatever you just did in reverse. Decide to do the idea you threw away last. Remove the last element you added. Don't fix the last mistake you made.

409

Celebrate someone's beauty, e.g., "You Are So Beautiful" by Billy Preston and Bruce Fisher. (Joe Cocker *cries* on the recording of that song.) John Lennon wrote "Julia" for his mother, and he cries on that tape, too. Maybe you can find somebody or something that makes you cry because they're so beautiful. Those would be good tears . . . and good songs, too.

410

Finish these phrases:

Why, I oughta _____.

Don't you think it's time we _____?

Especially when _____.

Baby, please _____.

You'll be _____.

The minute I _____.

I just want to _____.

Go on and _____.

It's still _____.

Rockin' and a _____.

Everybody _____.

Don't you _____.

It's the _____.

We can _____.

Where do _____?

Love is _____.

You give me _____.

It's too late for _____.

People say _____.

Only a fool would _____.

All because _____.

Remember the night we _____?

It was almost _____.

For the first time, I _____.

Here is _____.

What a way to _____.

Whenever we're together _____.

I miss _____.

How I wish _____.

We weren't even _____.

411

What will you wear and what kind of car will you drive when you have
your big hit song? What will your new friends and relatives be called?
"And to my cousin Alfred, who said I'd never mention him
in my will . . . 'Hi, Alfred!' "

412

"The Duke of Earl" (Eugene Dixon, Bernice Williams, and Earl Edwards), "The Duke of Dubuque" (Billy Faber, Janus Marchant, and Royal Lawrence), "The Sultans of Swing" (Mark Knopfler). Maybe you know somebody who likes to strut their stuff. Maybe they're nobility or royalty or just a royal pain. Maybe like Paul Simon's Speedo in "Was a Sunny Day" ("but his Christian name was Mr. Earl"), they just expect to be treated that way. My favorite song in this line of thinking is Don Henry's: ("That's") "Mr. God" ("to you!").

413

Try writing in notation. Make lead sheets part of your writing process. Use manuscripts to help you visualize your melody. Try the latest manuscripting software or something really bizarre, like lute tablature. Put a light show together.

414

Write a raga, using quarter tones. Music for a muezzin, the Feast of Ramadan, etc.

415

Start your story in some unlikely location. How about the swamp? Examples: "Jeremiah was a bullfrog" ("Joy to the World," Hoyt Axton), "Born on the Bayou" (John Fogerty), "Blue Bayou" (Roy Orbison), "Polk Salad Annie" (Tony Joe White). Tenements, dives, jungles, bars, dens of iniquity, and places of ill repute . . . You wouldn't want to take your mama to meet your "Private Dancer" (Mark Knopfler) or "Louise" (Paul Siebel), but you probably wouldn't mind if everybody else did (in a song). Songs are great ways to muckrake (or go slumming).

416

"Happiness Is a Thing Called Joe" (E. Y. "Yip" Harburg and Harold Arlen). "Happiness Is a Warm Gun" (Lennon and McCartney). Define happiness. Here are some people who have written songs to the title "Happy": Dick Seigel, George Michael, Mick Jagger and Keith Richards, William Bell, and Michel Legrand. Maybe you could add to their number. "Don't Worry, Be Happy!" (Bobby McFerrin).

417

Incite a jam session. Start a seance. Fill a punch bowl. Inaugurate a pillow fight. Cheer a football team. Break out a keg. Launch a ship.

418

Imagine some real or imaginary conflagrations. What's burning up? The obvious cliché is bridges. But there's also "Burning My Old Rowboat" (Larry Tagg).

419

What have you always wanted to write a song about but haven't yet?

420

Write a nostalgia piece. A plant can't put down its roots if it's always moving. Most of us don't know our neighbors the way our parents and grandparents knew theirs. What have we lost in our mobile society? What else?

421

Write a song about angels.

422

Put the ending first. Swap first and second verses. Uh . . . stand on your head? Yoga is a reliable day starter. Vary your work habits. Write at a different time of day than you have before. Shoehorn some time in on a weekly basis for your writing.

423

What are you in danger of becoming?
Doing? Having? Running away from?

424

Regarding unfinished business and/or
moving on; finish these phrases:

I never got over _____.
I still try to _____.
You're the reason _____.
I wish I could tell you _____.
How can I _____?
Except for _____.
Until today _____.
I'll never forget _____.
By now I should _____.
Every so often I _____.
No matter where I go _____.
I guess it wasn't _____.
Sometimes you just have to _____.
But when it's all said and done _____.

425

Use a bass line to walk down in this (hip) progression: 1→♭7→♭6→5, like:
"Hit the Road, Jack" (Ray Charles)
"Stray Cat Strut" (Brian Setzer)
"Steppin' Out With My Baby" (Irving Berlin)
"Sixteen Tons" (Merle Travis)

426

Waterways I have known. Snow. Rain.
Rivers I have crossed. Seas I have sailed.

427

And we weren't even *in* that mood! Surprise us.

428

That's ridiculous! Absurd! Surreal! Comical! Out of the *question.*

429

Oranges and apples. What *can't* you compare?

430

The last thing that I'd ever do is _____.

431

How could you prove you love somebody? *Is* there any way?

432

Make a list of intentions. What do you value most?
What will "stay with you" 'til the end?

433

Capture the way something moves: a belly dancer, a snake,
a carousel full of children.

434

Sit still and listen. Look up at the sky and depict clouds, birds, shafts of
sunlight, treetops, rooftops, the lines of airplane exhaust or the things they
remind you of.

435

Investigate the darker side of Miss Goody Two Shoes.

436

It's my boo-hoo-birth-hic-day . . . waaah! e.g., "Happy Birthday,
Dear Heartache" (Mack David and Archie Jordan), "Happy Birthday, Darlin' "
(Harlan Howard), "Sixteen Candles" (Luther Dixon and Allyson Khent),
"Forty-Five Years" (Stan Rogers). Put a little pathos into this occasion marking
your advancing years. After all, you're the *only* one who's ever
had a blue birthday, right?

437

Get your song criticized. Get turned down by a record label, an
artist, a producer, or a publisher. Watch the GRAMMY Awards, the
CMAs, or the Academy Awards. Eat your heart out that you're not
there, that you didn't win, or that you only won one. I think
rewriting is overrated. If song X isn't working for you, write song Y,
or rewrite song X; pirate parts of song X for song Y (heck, yes, you
can't plagiarize from yourself); or keep song X around for laughs.
But song X could inspire you to write song Y. Turn down my song
will you? Hah! (We'll show *them*, won't we?) Put down that Uzi.
Pick up a pen. Write another song. Out of the ashes, the phoenix
rises. Or write about that concept, the coming back to haunt the
unbelievers. O, ye of little faith!

Let disappointment and rejection fuel your creativity. The "I'll
show them" factor has spurred many a creative moment. The
numbers of writers and artists who came from schools or
publishers or families who didn't appreciate them or who were
downright dysfunctional is legion. But this doesn't have to be a sad
comment on approval-seeking adults. This can be the way and the
reason that wounds become gifts. These are spiritual gifts of
sensitivity, empathy, self-expression, channeling, and transforming
ugliness into beauty.

Let disgust fuel your creativity, too. "I can do better than that" has
inspired many a creative effort. If you disagree with prevailing
norms, customs, musical styles, attitudes, or the quality of
somebody else's music, offer a tangible alternative.

438

"The Very Thought of You, My Dear" (Ray Noble).
Who turns your mind into jelly?

439

Swear a little, e.g., "Darn That Dream" (Jimmy van Heusen and
Edgar deLange). How about: "Dang Me" (". . . they oughtta take a
rope and hang me . . . ") (Roger Miller).

440

"What Are You Doing New Year's Eve?" (Frank Loesser). Good question. Make some promises or resolutions or plans and talk about them in your song, e.g., "I Swear" (Gary Baker and Frank Myers).

441

Tell 'em how you like 'em, e.g., "Any Man of Mine" (Faith Hill), "Do That to Me One More Time" (Toni Tennille).

442

Some jazz greats: Charlie Parker, Thelonious Monk, Charles Mingus, Louis Armstrong, Django Reinhardt (just reminding you). They each had characteristic improvisational styles that can be studied and imitated. Of course, you can't copy my E note, because I own that one, but you're welcome to the others. No, I think D7 is trademarked also.

443

Write an elegy.

444

Write a mystery play referring to dynamic Biblical duos: Adam and Eve, Essau and Jacob, Samson and Delilah, David and Goliath, Abraham and Isaac. Or what about the moment of revelation, the great conflict, etc. Perhaps another text, such as *Autobiography of a Yogi*, has something for you. Pick a creation myth, a Sufi story, a teaching koan, or a parable, and set it to music.

445

Scare yourself. Go bungee jumping; go sky diving. Give a speech. Visit a rest home. Ask for a raise. Ask for an autograph. Call up your old teacher and thank him or her. In other words, if you're living at the edge of yourself, your creative chances are greater. So go do something hard. An open mic? A poetry reading? A hair-raising movie? A marriage proposal? (Not recommended more than once.)

446

Restrict yourself. Don't use the tonic (one-chord) anywhere in the song.

447

Never go to the five-chord in the song (this is surprisingly hard).

448

Write out the shape of your melody on a piece of paper in dark ink. Turn the paper over and trace a melody that goes in the opposite direction. Then fold the paper over and do the same thing. Put your high notes where your low notes are, or put your high notes at a different place in the structure of the melody. (There's more about this technique in the appendix.)

449

Write a song about being in a hurry or having plenty of time.

450

What's easy? What's hard? About growing up, loving, leaving, getting over somebody or something?

451

This is an idea I heard from Pierce Pettis, who said he got it from John Stewart: Put your head between at least two and up to six loudspeakers broadcasting different types of music at once. Apparently this scrambles your music processing, so that you get a kind of juicy noise pool from which to write a new melody.

452

Go to a play. Go to an art gallery. Go to a museum.
A petting zoo? A paint store?

453

Study fortune cookies, cereal boxes, coupons,
and other pieces of "found" poetry.

454

Picture your favorite relative and describe one of their quirks.
What? They don't have any? That's quirky.

455

What are your (forgivable) foibles? Your beloved belongings?

456

Consider the migrations of your ancestors. Why did they go? What were they
after? What did they find? "A people without history is like wind on the buffalo
grass" (Sioux proverb). How did your parents meet? Grandparents? Are there
any romantic family stories to preserve in song? Stories of family heroism? Any
black sheep in your family?

457

Pebbles and pearls. "That Was a River" ("this is the ocean")
(Susan Longacre and Richard Giles). Compare the value of a relationship or
what you know about love "now" with what you knew "then."

458

Counterfeit a musical tradition. Write a sea chantey, a Childe ballad recently
discovered (penned by you, of course), or a shape note song. Maybe the
heyday of that music has passed, but maybe you could revive interest in it
by adding to the tradition.

459

Wayne Carson once wrote a song that says, "We're alike as two snowflakes." You expected him to say "peas in a pod" maybe? To me, there are three different levels of cleverness in lyric writing. Level one is where a pun is in the title. Level two is where a whole line of the song is used in the service of a pun. But level three, the quintessential level of skill, is where puns are imbedded in the song in such a way that you don't even register them. It's not just a play on words, it's playing with irony at a much deeper level. Wayne has a song like that. He talks about traveling through Snowflake, Arizona, and then way down in the middle of the second verse, he says he doesn't have a chance in hell of getting his woman back. You connect the dots yourself. See if you can aim for level three. You might get two, but you'll never get to three if you don't know it's there to aim for.

460

Get theatrical and fool around with your instrument. (That's probably why they call it "playing" music as opposed to "working" music.) If you play guitar, try damping down, pulling off, hammering on, using harmonics, or slapping the body of the guitar as part of your song. If God had intended us just to *strum* the guitar, guitars would be nothing but strings.

461

Here is the chord chart of a progression used by "Hound Dog" (Jerry Leiber and Mike Stoller); "Blue Suede Shoes" (Carl Perkins); "Jailhouse Rock" (Leiber and Stoller); "Oh, Carol" (Howard Greenfield and Neil Sedaka); "Mabelline," "Sweet Little Sixteen," "Memphis, Tennessee," "Johnny B. Goode," "Roll Over, Beethoven," and "Rock and Roll Music" (all by Chuck Berry). *(Your song's name here.)*

1 1 1 1
4 4 1 1
5 4 1 1

462

George Brassens, the great French lyricist, made great use of one-noun titles. These can be very evocative, e.g., the Philistines, the gorilla, the orange, the wind, the bicycle, the garden, the gravedigger. Try wrapping your story around a single noun.

463

Celebrate music itself. "I've Got the Music in Me!" (Bias Boshell), ("there'll be") "Sad Songs" ("to make you cry") (Bernie Taupin and Elton John), "I Write the Songs" (Bruce Johnston), "It's Still Rock and Roll to Me" (Billy Joel).

464

John Calvi played an icebreaker game at the Quaker Center last year with a group of us. Maybe his questions will spark something in you, too:
What is your secret addiction?
Who would your three Supreme Court nominees be?
If you could have coffee with anybody, who would it be?
If you could travel around the world for a year with someone you didn't like, who would it be?
If you could send a message to world leaders, what would it be?
What's the worst thing you've heard in a meeting?
If you had one million dollars to spend by tomorrow, how would you spend it?
Tell something you've told no one else.
Name a new hotel.
What was your best or worst high school moment?
What was the best fun you ever had in a car?
Whose house guest would you like to be?
What's the best gift you could get?
What's your most unQuaker-like desire?
What's the worst insult you ever uttered in anger?
What's the biggest lie you ever told?
If you could steal one thing and keep it, what would it be?

465

Write a song about a hotel or motel, e.g., "Third-Rate Romance" (Howard Russell Smith), "Heartbreak Hotel" (Mae Axton, Elvis Presley, and Tommy Durden), "Hotel California" (Don Felder, Don Henley, and Glenn Frey). What about a restaurant, bar, waitress (e.g., "The Lady Who Carries the Tray" [Chuck McCabe]), waiter, cook, pearl diver.

466

What would people see if you really did live in a glass house?

467

Hold yourself in your own arms. What is the kindest, gentlest, most merciful song you could make for yourself?

468

What cause would you champion in a song?

469

Imagine you died yesterday. Write your own obituary. What accomplishments, relationships meant the most? Who would care most if you died? Comfort them.

470

Describe a wilderness.

471

Write a song about a secret initiation.

472

What did your parents never do? Are you a chip off the old block? Were you or should you have been adopted? Write a song for your dad or mother. If there are unresolved issues or your parents aren't around, you still have plenty to say, right?

473
When did you cease to be a child?

474
Write for your mentors and well-wishers. Who has enriched your life, cared, challenged, taught, and delighted in you?

475
Have you ever had any close calls?

476
Finish these phrases:

No matter how long I live _____.

No matter how hard you try _____.

No matter what anybody says _____.

How much more _____ will it take?

There's a heavy price to pay for _____.

It's so hard to _____.

It's so good to _____.

I always know when _____.

477
Should you or shouldn't you? Will you or won't you?
Stand at the crossroads and explore your options.

478
Write a song for group spirit, a revival, a communion, an offertory, a "last supper" (or a first dinner on the ground).

479
Anticipate or suspend chords using a 4th above from one chord to another, such as C7sus4 above C7 to resolve upward at F. Replace root triads (1 3 5 chords) with sustained chords (1 4 5 chords).

480

Use some chord inversions. Put at least one chord extension
(9ths, 11ths, 13ths chords) into your arrangement.

481

Try writing in a song form you haven't tried before. If you haven't
written a song *without* a chorus, try that; or if you haven't written a
song *with* a chorus, try that.

482

Write a melody that progresses in waves, with each melodic
shape higher than the last and each group of note values shorter
than the last. In other words, speed up and lift your melody to hit
a climax. Write a melody that soars.

483

Pretend you're Picasso. How would a Cubist tell your story? What are
the facets and angular juxtapositions of ideas you could use? Put your eyeball
on your shoulder.

484

Doesn't it feel good to be *alone* sometimes? Turn some assumed or accepted
cliché on its head. For instance, alone doesn't have to be lonely. Or maybe
there's no such thing as love at first sight; there's only love that is developed
over time. Maybe you know some teenager who likes hanging out with his
parents, or a really sweet mother-in-law, or a saintly (instead of wicked)
stepmother. Or maybe you feel there is no honor among thieves, not all is fair
in love and war, the weaker sex is the stronger, or nice guys finish first. Show
how your life differs from the cliché.

485

Write on shelf paper, a grocery sack, extra long legal pads. If you're right-handed, use your left hand to write. Write from the bottom of the page upward or from outward in. Use the margins. Sit in your chair backwards. Squat or lie on the floor. Draw your lyrics in the dirt with a stick or imagine them on the ceiling. Write tiny characters. Write big. Use *crayons*. Write in a spiral. Write in clusters. Draw cartoons to illustrate your lyrics. Take up space . . .

S P A C E
P
A
C
E

486

Write a campfire song or a song for summer camp, as in this classic:
"Hello Mudduh, Hello Fadduh
(Here I am at Camp Granada
Camp is very entertaining
And the counselors say we'll have some fun if it stops raining)"
—Allan Sherman and Louis F. Bush

487

I recently heard Utah Phillips say something truly empowering to a group of singer-songwriters: "Don't give 'em what they want to hear. Give 'em what *you* want them to hear."

488

Write a call-and-response song, where a line is sung and then answered by a group. These are community-based songs, especially prevalent in religious music and the African musical tradition. They're also powerful in establishing solidarity, forever.

489

Make faces while you sing. Play charades with your song title.

490

If you had a lost and found for dreams,
what old dreams would show up in it?

491

Write a song before you're ready to.

492

Paint without a brush. Start a fire without matches.

493

When was the last time your teacher/preacher/pop icon acted human?
How were they diminished in a moment of weakness or tenderness?

494

Spit it out. No, no, not your gum, silly! The truth you've been saving.

495

I got a huge kick out of writing a blues song with Betsy Jackson and
Karen Taylor Good called "Brain Surgeon." (One lyric went: "I'm a brain
surgeon, baby; I want to play with your mind . . . ") How richly rewarding
it was to later meet and play this for a friend of mine who happens to
be—you guessed it—a brain surgeon! Think of a song that would be
perfect for a particular person or occasion, and if possible, lay it on 'em.
Yes, Richard Leigh wrote huge hits, including "Don't It Make My Brown
Eyes Blue" and "Somewhere in My Broken Heart," but his most
requested song? "The Night They Made the First Cub Scout," in honor
of the Blue and Gold Awards Banquet. Go, Bobcats! Hooray, Webelos!
You can make yourself useful or zot right into the heart of a person or a
community with a song. Some friend of yours is having a tough time? A
baby? A moral dilemma? Falling out of love? Falling in love? A crisis of
faith? You can be right there with them.

496

Think of great collaborative relationships, e.g., Leiber and Stoller, Kelly and Steinberg, Mann and Weil, George and Ira Gershwin. Find out about them. Imagine imitating their styles and processes. Pretend you're working in a stormy, Gilbert and Sullivan relationship, where you both remain at arm's length. Collaborate via the mail, over the telephone, or at a prescribed time. At home. In a publisher's office. Try collaborating if you haven't. Divide up responsibilities or have a free-for-all dialogue. Respect each other and give each other's ideas some room. If possible, love each other and let your writing speak volumes on quality intimacy and friendship.

497

Clip pictures and articles about things you love and are working toward: vacations, new careers, children, etc. Or you can use souvenirs and photographs to help you remember your dreams and fond memories; these will become a part of your songs.

498

What are places you've always wanted to visit? Do something you never got to do as a kid. Ride a roller coaster. Stay up all night. Climb a tree. Jump on the bed. Mess up a pile of raked leaves. Have a food, water, shaving cream, whipped cream, or marshmallow fight in the kitchen. Invest in a whoopee cushion. (I got this idea from Doug Hall.)

499

Write a song about keeping silence, e.g., ("you say it best") "When You Say Nothing at All" (Don Schlitz and Paul Overstreet).

500

What the heck—get some sleep. Do some living. If you drop this writing/"self expression" and do more listening, reading, and quietly taking stuff in, you'll probably have a jillion ideas tomorrow. Sometimes you have to allow for the ebb as well as the flow. Let yourself have a fallow field so you can grow some beauties tomorrow. Don't call it writer's block. Call it writer's rest, or input versus output time, or making a living, or being a mom or dad, or doing something else that might take precedence. It's okay.
It may be stupid, but you dare to be stupid, right?

Appendix

There are five main elements, or tools, useful in songwriting: *form, melody, harmony, rhythm,* and *lyrics.* Because of this, I structured my course at PSGW to discuss these topics, in this order, one on each of the five days of my songwriting class. What follows is part of the course material. Don't be spooked if it looks technical. This is partly a glossary to help you find your way through the words in the idea section and partly a short introduction to songwriting per se. The words in the glossary aren't alphabetized, rather I've placed them in the order in which people are most likely to encounter these elements when they're writing a song. If you get a handle on these concepts, you can write songs. They're like building blocks: Put one down and see where you can stack the next one. But I wouldn't dream of telling you *how* to write a song. I honestly don't know, and if I did know, I wouldn't say. Why? Because it would be a terrible box in which to put yourself if there were a recipe or an algorithm that you had to follow. Fortunately, there's no such thing. You're safe from pedagogy. Songwriting is nestled in the heart of creativity, where it belongs.

I have some unusual ways of conceptualizing this material. The way I write songs is a bit of a curiosity. People sometimes wonder how a musical ignoramus, a person who doesn't play an instrument, could compose songs. So, I've included a section about my own writing process that appears after this appendix. Of course, I'm also indebted to many wonderful musicians and co-writers who've helped me actualize songs. But it's not just sour grapes to say that you don't need musicians to hear your music. You don't need a lot of "background." Waiting for yourself to be sufficiently prepared, for the day when you're really *qualified* to write songs—that day may never come, even with a Ph.D. in music. *Be* unready. Allow for imperfection. Remain open to chaos. Your education can get in the way of your creativity. Ask any hardened veteran of grade school! Did you play more in kindergarten or 12th grade? Most of us would answer the former, but what we *need* is recess for adults. So, take the "educational" part of this book with a grain of salt. The appendix is here to help, not hinder, your playing. It's really recess time, not class time, that makes the difference.

Lingo Regarding Song Form

Hook: the catchy part of a song.

Title: the name of the song; it often has the hook in it.

Chorus: the melodically repeated part of a song. The chorus is the "goal" of the song that sums it up or reflects the theme. The chorus usually has the hook in it. Because this is almost always the focal point of a song, it can be quicker to write it first and then backtrack to the other sections.

First verse: the section that motivates or sets up the situation or storyline that leads to the chorus.

Second verse: the plot thickens. The continuation of the storyline or another angle of approach to the chorus. Almost always musically identical to the first verse.

Bridge: a breath of fresh air, melodically and lyrically different from the rest of the song. The bridge takes a different tack on the song idea. For instance, if the rest of the song is narrative and personal in tone, the bridge might be more philosophical in tone; or if the rest of the song is slow, the bridge might be faster. Frequently the bridge is signaled by a change in key that ramps the song up energetically into the last rousing chorus.

Intro: instrumental introduction to a song often containing part or all of a verse.

Outro: also known as the "tag"; instrumental conclusion to a song, often the same as the intro.

Song Forms:

If   A = a verse

and B = a chorus or the next different section from the one preceding it,

and C = a bridge or the next different section from the one preceding it, here are some typical song forms:

ABAB: usually country or folk style, e.g., "O, Susannah."

ABABCB: the most common form; country, pop, and R&B style, e.g., Billy Cobham's "Soul Provider."

Intro, ABABCAB, outro: pop, rock, jazz; such as "Waiting for a Star to Fall" (George Merrill and Shannon Rubicam).

AA'BAA'BCB: a common pop and rock style where A' is a repeated change in a verse, or *pre-chorus*, as in the Bee Gees' "High As a Mountain."

AABA: jazz and pop, e.g., "Yesterday" (Paul McCartney).

ABAC: jazz, for example, "All of Me" (Seymour Simons and Gerald Marks).

AAA: blues and bluegrass, e.g., "In the Pines" (Leadbelly).

BABAB: of course you can start with the chorus, but make sure it's not like giving away the punch line of a joke. Example: "Chain of Fools" (Donald Covay).

A song that has no chorus and one "A" section is called *through composed*. "I Remember Sky" by Stephen Sondheim is one example. "The Chair" by Dean Dillon and Hank Cochran is another. And of course, there are many form variations. For unusual song forms, check out They Might Be Giants, The B-52's, Nina Hagen, Annie Lennox, Joni Mitchell, Seal, Hootie and the Blowfish, and Prince.

Lingo Regarding Melody

Motif: a sequence of two to eight notes; a little kernel of melody. Some ways to vary the motif while still staying close to it so that it is recognizable are:

Retrograde: reversing the motif (i.e., making it bilaterally symmetrical across the vertical axis).

Inversion: turning the motif upside down (i.e., making it bilaterally symmetrical across the horizontal axis).

Transposition: lifting or lowering the whole motif by starting on a different place in the scale. For example, the first three notes of the melody of "Three Blind Mice" are repeated and transposed in the next line, "See how they run."

In the following diagram:
O = the original melody
R = the retrograde melody
I = the inverted melody
R + I = both reversed and inverted melody

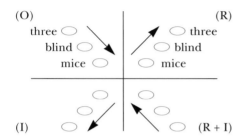

As you can see, this is a wonderful way to play with and change melodies. If the notes go up, try going down. Go up or down by the same amount or make intervals from the same starting point, down or up to the same starting point. "Somewhere Over the Rainbow" by Yip Harburg and Harold Arlen is an example of a melodic motif being turned around and played with throughout a piece. How about "Bottle of Wine" by Tom Paxton? Beethoven's 5th Symphony? Motifs that recur give unity and integrity to a piece of music. But they don't have to be repeated exactly to sound familiar.

Scale: stepwise motion between notes, up or down the scale.

Interval: the jumps between notes.

What our ears are used to hearing in Western music is arranged in a system of intervals that follow a pattern of whole steps between every note except notes three to four and seven to eight, which are half steps. So, counting up the scale (with uppercase roman numerals to indicate dominant tones):

1	2	3	4	5	6	7	8 or 1
do	re	mi	fa	sol	la	ti	do
I	ii	iii	IV	V	vi	vii	I

The intervals are whole step, whole step, half step, whole step, whole step, whole step, half step. In the key of C, the notes are C D E F G A B C, where the second C is an octave above the first.

Key: the 1, bottom, or "root" of the scale; this determines the key. Flats and sharps are used to preserve the stepwise pattern of intervals while changing keys.

Flats: going down a half step, except when the interval is already a half step between the notes. For instance, in the key of C, we say C to B and F to E, we don't have "C flat," because this is B (see *Interval*).

Sharps: going up a half step, except when the interval is already a half step between notes. We don't say E to F is "E sharp," because this is F (see *Interval*).

Natural: when a note in the key is made to fit the pattern of steps without any sharps or flats.

Accidental: a note that occurs in a piece of music outside its key.

Enharmonic: on the same pitch (sound) of the note.

Chromatic: moving up and down the scale by half steps.

Diatonic: the melody moves up and down the scale with no sharps or flats. In C major, those notes would be all the white keys on a piano: C D E F G A B C.

Tessatura: the highest note in the piece.

Lingo Regarding Harmony
Third: two notes that are two notes away from each other. The higher note is a third up. A major third is two steps away. A minor third is 1½ steps away.

Triad: three notes forming a chord.

Tetrachord: four notes forming a chord.

Major triad: two whole steps and 1½ steps, or a major third and a minor third. Example in the key of C: C E G, (C).

Minor triad: 1½ steps and two steps, or a minor third and a major third. Example in the key of C: C E♭ G, (C min).

Dominant seventh: example in the key of C: C E G B♭, (C7).

Major seventh: example in the key of C: C E G B, (Cmaj7).

Minor seventh: example in the key of C: C E♭ G B♭, (Cmin7).

Diminished triad: flat (½ step down) both the nonroot notes of the triad.
Example in the key of C: C E♭ G♭, (Cdim).

Diminished seventh: flat (½ step down) all the notes in the dominant seventh
     but the root.
Example in the key of C: C E♭ G♭ A, (Cdim7, C°, sometimes Cdim).

Augmented triad: sharp (½ step up) the third note of the triad (two stacked
     major thirds).
Example in the key of C: C E G#, (C+).

Augmented seventh: sharp (½ step up) the third note of the dominant seventh
     chord.
Example in the key of C: C E G# B♭, (C7+).

Circle of 5ths: (really the circle of 4ths) is a way of cycling through key
changes, so that each position in the circle is four notes away from the next
one; you are either moving up a fourth or down a fifth. The circle is a cycle of
dominant or 5 (V) chords. C is the V chord of F, which is the V chord of B♭,
which is the V chord of G, which is the V chord of C, and so on. The relative
minor is the note ¼ turn of the circle to the right. The relative minor has the
same number of accidentals as its relative major. As you go around the circle,
you add one accidental per key.

Modulation: changing key; also called *transposition.*

Enharmonic modulation: the whole scale transposed up or down but changing
keys that share that note. A nifty, common way to modulate from one key to
another is to progress gradually, e.g., 1→2→5→1 in the new key.

Mode: the whole scale transposed up or down but preserving the pattern of intervals. The arrangement of whole steps and half steps is moved to a different starting place, but the intervals between the sol and fa syllables, or notes, remains constant. The notes referred to in describing the following modes are those used in the C major scale (the white keys on a piano, no sharps or flats):

> Aeolian: the minor mode, starts and ends on "la" (A).
> Dorian: starts and ends on "re" (D).
> Ionian: the typical major mode, the one our ears are used to hearing, starting and ending on "do" (C).
> Locrian: starts and ends on "ti" (B).
> Lydian: starts and ends on "fa" (F).
> Mixolydian: starts and ends on "sol" (G).
> Phrygian: starts and ends on "mi" (E).

Nashville Notation: a way of writing down chords without respect to key signature, in terms of relative intervals. The tonic or root chord of a key is 1, 2 is the chord one step up from that, 3 is the third, and so on up the scale. Usually, 4/4 time is assumed unless otherwise noted, so the chords are written in groups of four.

> Superscripts mean the following:
> "$^-$" means minor, so 6 is a "six minor" chord. In the key of C, that would be Amin.
> "^{o}" means diminished.
> "$^+$" means augmented.
> "$^\Delta$" means major with a dominant seventh, or the "7th" chord.

A chord that is written with a diagonal line and another number denotes the chord and its bass note. For example, "1/3" means a 1 chord with a 3 bass note. In the key of C, that would be C with an E in the bass.

A chord that is written with a vertical line and another number denotes a split bar. For example: In 4/4 time, "1|5" means two beats of the 1 chord and two beats of the 5 chord.

A diamond shape around a number indicates a whole note over the chord.

Here's a sample chord chart for a song of mine called " 'Til the Cows Come Home," arranged by Jamey Whiting and Howard Schwartz. It's written to be played in the key of D, and it has two separate endings:

(D)
'Til the Cows Come Home

INTRO:		1/6-	2-/5	1/6-	2-/5
VERSE:		1	1	4	3-
		4	1/6-	2	5
CHORUS:		4	1	4	3-
		4	1/6-	2-/5	
TURNAROUND:	(1)	1/6-	2-/5		
	(2)	1/5			
VERSE:		1	1	4	3-
		4	1/6-	2	5
CHORUS:		4	1	4	3-
		4	1/6-	2-/5	
TAGS:		1/6-	2-/5		
		1/6	2-/5		

(FADE)

Lingo Regarding Rhythm

Rhythm is the pattern of beats. Tempo is how fast they are played within the units of rhythm, measures, or bars. Here are some sample rhythms or meters and their dance styles:

$\frac{4}{4}$ The most common time, sometimes written "C":

4 ← beats per measure
4 ← quarter note gets the count of one beat

Back beat: the "up" beats, e.g., One AND two AND (i.e., beats 2 and 4 of a song in 4/4).

Typically, the back beats are the ANDs.

Some 4/4 dances can be found in rock and roll, as well as the rumba, the fox trot, the cha cha.

$\frac{2}{2}$ This rhythm is divisible by twos, or duple; a gavotte (even and slow).

$\frac{2}{4}$ Also achieved by "cutting time" of 4/4 in half to feel faster.
Examples: Morris dance, paso doble, tango, reel, hornpipe, polka, marches.

$\frac{3}{4}$ This rhythm is divisible by threes, or triple. Viennese waltzes emphasizes
the downbeat. Cajun waltzes emphasize all three beats. In jazz waltzes,
beat 2 is pushed early:
<u>3</u>←beats per measure
4←quarter note gets the count of one beat. Examples: waltz, mazurka,
polka-waltz.

Some 8 to the bar timings are: 6/8, 12/8 (exemplified by a lot of Fats Domino's
songs), and 8/8 (e.g., jig, two-step, tarantella). A slip jig is in 9/8 time. These
rhythms can be accented in threes *or* twos, so they can give rise to interesting
combinations.

In the following notation, a dot signifies a rest, a number signifies a beat, and
a letter "e" or "a" signifies a count that is off the beat.

A shuffle has triplets that leave out the middle of each group of three notes in
a four-beat phrase—e.g., 1 · a 2 · a 3 · a 4 ·, dragging over the first note 2/3 the
duration of the phrase and having the last note 1/3 the duration of the phrase.
If you were walking to this, a shuffle would be a limp.

A half-time shuffle, hip hop, or jack swing is in triplets:
1 e a and e a 2 e a and e a 3 e a and e a 4 e a and e a.
Or in shuffle time:
1 · a and · a 2 · a and · a 3 · a and · a 4 · a and · a.

I learned this partly from Cat Cohen and partly from dancing to a lot of
rap and disco myself. As music becomes more rhythmically sophisticated, it of course, tends to borrow from other cultures. African, Cuban,
and Brazilian music have several grooves layered and alternating on top
of one another.

Salsa is a combination of triplets over 4/4: 123, 123 . . . and · 123, · 12,
· 123, · 12.

Sixteen beats to the bar (four notes per beat) is most common in modern rock, rap, pop, R&B, and country rock writing: 1 e and a 2 e and a 3 e and a 4 e and a.

There are lots of unusual rhythms in Balkan dancing: 5/4, 3/2, 5/8, 7/8, even 5/9 is not uncommon.

N.B. Get 'em DANCING!

Lingo Regarding Lyrics
Lyrics are not literary; they are auditory. Sound über sense! Poetry is different from lyrics in that lyrics are intended to be sung. As such, the first thing to check out in a lyric is its singability. Long vowels, especially "ay," "I," "ooh," and diphthongs (two or more vowels together), at the ends of lines make for more singable lyrics. Using lots of short vowels and consonants creates a more percussive lyric with more emphasis and abruptness. This is especially appropriate in R&B or rock lyrics where the message may be urgent or aggressive.

Some Useful Poetic Devices:
Alliteration: same beginnings of words.

Assonance: same vowel sounds of words.

Parallel structure: one part of the lyric uses the same grammatical structure as another (e.g., using a list versus subject/predicate form).

Rhyme: same sounds of words in a continuum of perfect matching to near-rhymes or assonance. How many rhymes you use affects the speed of the line delivery. Lots of inner rhymes or multiple-syllable rhymes gives a fast, light effect to a lyric. Unusual rhymes are sometimes funny: "skeleton" and "gelatin" is funnier than "heart" and "apart" and might belong in a Broadway-style piece because of its cleverness.

Scope: The scope of the language uses parallel structure, too. For example, you'd compare apples and oranges but not apples and fruit because fruit is a set that contains apples and is more general than apples. Similarly, you wouldn't have a prizefighter talk like a ten-year-old girl. Lyrics pay attention to the character and point of view of the speaker. What they talk about and how they talk about it is their "universe of discourse." Make sure you keep consistency in that department, as well as who is speaking and when, throughout the song.

Scansion, or scanning: how the accents fall on the syllables of words to achieve a rhythmic pattern.

Prosody: how the words fit the music. Usually good scansion results in good prosody.

Inflections: When putting a melody to a lyric, read it out loud first and see how the rising and falling inflections or the emphases you place on certain syllables give rise to pitches and rhythms. The natural drama of ordinary speech is musical. Use the following symbols to diagram your inflections:

/	=	accented sound
U	=	unaccented sound
/U	=	trochee
U/	=	iamb
/U U	=	dactyl
U U/	=	anapest
//	=	spondee

Metrical feet: the number of groups of syllables in a phrase. For example, iambic pentameter = 5 "feet" of iambs.

Put words or phrases together that sound like the rhythms you want to remember and repeat them:

Butternut squash	/UU/
Ricochet	/U/
One more cup of soup	UU/U/
There you go, cowboy	/U//U
It's easy for you to say	UUUU/U/
Slow down, son	///
Talk with the elephant, walk with the elephant	/UU/UU,/UU/UU
Remember believing	U/U U/U
Sentimental journey	/U/U/U

Regarding My Own Songwriting Process

My writing process is more like digital filtering than synthesis. This means I often work with my mental library and tease out, or do signal conditioning, on sound, rather than building it block by block from scratch. In other words, I work like a digital filter, which starts with noise and pulls out frequencies of interest, rather than adding sine waves. I use the songs I've already heard—I have a huge mental library to draw from—and I transform and deform those sounds. Without formal training in music, I use my informal training instead. I use my "inner hearing."

Inner hearing requires a certain amount of memory for melody. You can train yourself to do this in the same fashion that you might train your spatial abilities, i.e., by holding melody in your "inner ear." (In spatial thinking, this would be analogous to imagining a picture in your "mind's eye.") Yes, these faculties do exist! See the amazing work of Stanford cognitive psychologist Roger Shepherd if you don't believe me!

Recall notes or tunes you just heard and see how many you can put together in a row. In my class at P.S.G.W., I asked people to sing their names to each other, playing with add-ons. Most songs have a signature motif or hook to help you remember them. Once you can remember melodies, see if you can hold them in your head long enough to change them.

I use Cartesian graphs and other geometrical models of my melodies, and I generally play with melodic motifs as logical units, rather than with single notes. (See "Lingo Regarding Melody" in the appendix for some ways to play with motifs.)

In film scoring, typically whole passages will be linked to a character or some action, and then those blocks of music will be reprised and treated the same way melodic motifs are treated in songs. We write overtures. Repetition, repetition, repetition.

It's the better part of valor to stay on a note and sequence harmonies underneath, or change melodies stepwise, or use fewer notes, or use recognizable chord progressions. Who *says* you have to be sophisticated? I'm living proof that you can write songs with zero chops. Yes, Virginia, simplicity *is* a virtue.

I pay attention to bass lines to indicate arrangements, and I try to keep something stationary, either the bass line (as in Celtic music) or the melody note (as in Brazilian music). Bill Piburn taught me this. When I asked him how he wrote such wonderful melodies, he said that most people underestimate the power of staying where they are; they wander too much. See if you can stay a long time in one place melodically or harmonically while contrasting it with some other element that you change.

Writing a capella has low cartage (it's very portable) and it doesn't obfuscate melodic ideas by fancy arrangement ideas. I can tell if I'm staying on one note or boring myself. I can take my writing into the shower or down to the beach. And best of all, my melodies are more likely to be memorable because I have to remember them, and more likely to be singable because I sing them.

What I'm really trying to say in this book is don't wait to be a genius to write your songs—no hard feelings, geniuses. Just take a deep breath and *go* for it. What have you got to lose? Your pride? Pride schmide! Your dignity? Dignity schmignity! The undying respect and admiration of your family? Now *there's* a concept! On the other hand, just suppose that they don't go in for that kind of thing. Parents are rarely overjoyed by their musical offspring. You are still who you are, with or without anybody's permission or approval.

Sure, you're brave and passionate. You have to be to engage in any art whatsoever. I'm not talking about being an iconoclast; I'm talking about having integrity and the courage of your convictions. If you didn't have something to say, you wouldn't be doing this. But keep your eye on the birdy. There are small, selfish dreams and there are big ones. We can all be dreaming and living and loving more expansively. What are you waiting for? We've got stuff to do. I dare you.

Index

A Music Bookstore At Your Fingertips...

FREE!